CHRIST AND ADORNMENTS:

A Prize Essay, in Answer to the Inquiry,

WHAT IS THE MIND OF CHRIST WITH RESPECT TO CHRISTIANS ADORNING THEMSELVES WITH JEWELRY AND GAY AND COSTLY ATTIRE?

BY REV. S. H. PLATT.

CINCINNATI:
WESTERN TRACT AND BOOK SOCIETY,
No. 28 West Fourth Street.
1867.

CHRIST AND ADORNMENTS.

More than twelve hundred years ago a man of commanding presence, majestic aspect, and open countenance, "that painted every sensation of the soul," might have been seen fleeing for life, with a single attendant, from the rock-bound city of Mecca, in Arabia. Over nine weary miles had they rushed in despairing haste, when the approach of the foe warned them that flight was vain. At that critical juncture a friendly cave offered them its shelter, and they hastily concealed themselves within it. A bird immediately alighted upon a shrub at the opening, from which it was frightened by the arrival of the blood-thirsty pursuers. Seeing the bird fly, they inferred that if the fugitives had recently entered, it would have been driven away before, and not wishing to waste time in unnecessary search, they passed on and left

Mohammed in security. Thus, the flight of that bird changed the destiny of the world. It preserved the life of the false Prophet, and with him the reign of the superstition which he established, and which, after twelve centuries of effort, has nearly as wide an ascendency over the human race as Christianity itself.

This is one of the numerous instances recorded showing the most intimate and important relations between things totally dissimilar and apparently disconnected.

They reveal the fact that a complete isolation, such as would exclude us from the reciprocal influence of surrounding circumstances, is impossible. They also suggest the difficulty of forming any probable estimate of the results of any event, however trivial in its nature.

It is stated that a Welsh clergyman once asked a little girl for the text of his last sermon. The child's only reply was tears. He soon ascertained that she had no Bible in which to find the text. Upon further inquiry, he learned that the families around were in like destitution. This led him to apply to the committee of the Tract Society in London, for the adoption of some means to provide Bibles.

The result was the formation of the British and Foreign Bible Society, and through that, of all the other Bible Societies in the world.

Few would prophesy that the tears of a little girl would prove the prolific fountain of the Word of Life to the millions who have been supplied by the agency of Bible Societies; and fewer still would ever predict that the flight of a bird, so insignificant as a *cause*, would, in its results, rear a mighty monument of licentious superstition and cruel oppression over the pathway of the ages, shrouding the hearts of myriads in its shadow. Yet such are the strange, though not infrequent developments of history.

Around the pathway of every one, a variety of unexpected circumstances start up and weave themselves, whether we will or not, into the running web of our existence, and impart to it more or less of their own character. How often does the youth start upon the journey of life with his course mapped out before him, and with a strong determination never to swerve from his preconcerted plans. But some day he forms a new acquaintance, hears of some hitherto unknown object of desire, or is surrounded by some combination of unlooked for circumstances, and the whole current of his life is changed.

Amid such liabilities we all live; and were our life so pure that we could turn all effects, both great and small, by a divine alchemy, into the pure water of life, then were it well. But our nature is depraved; so depraved that it needs not the furnace heat to ignite its combustible material, or awaken its explosive power. A single spark will do as well.

No wonder then, that, surrounded as we are by all existing agencies of evil, the law of interinfluence that we have stated becomes a means of increasing our corruption, and spreading the ruin of our sins. But while it is thus rendered an instrument of evil, it has also become, in the hands of Divine mercy, an Evangelist of good, *for the design of the religion of Christ is to purify man's character in the use of the same law.* . . . "Even as Christ also loved the church, and gave himself for it, that he might sanctify and cleanse it with the washing of water by the word, that he might present it to himself a glorious church, not having spot, or wrinkle, or any such thing; but that it should be holy and without blemish," Eph. v: 26, 27. Here, purification of the character is expressly stated as the object of the atonement; and as this result can be realized only in the use of means, and as all means are subject to the same law, it follows that the law itself is subservient to that end.

Youth, by the impulsiveness of their nature, are peculiarly exposed to the warping power of surrounding influences, so that "trifles light as air" often become the ponderous weights which, when cast upon their life-scales, decide their future destiny. Surely a fact embracing such wide and commanding interests and far-reaching consequences, can not be lightly regarded by him whose precepts and example taught his disciples to "despise not the day of small things," for "behold how great a fire a little matter kindleth." The proposition may now be distinctly stated, that whatever is embraced by the great law of inter-influence is matter of interest to our Savior. And as the wearing of gold and costly attire is included, we may now ask, "What is the mind of Christ with respect to Christians adorning their persons with jewelry, and gay and costly attire; and what is the effect of such adorning upon the individual, the church, and the world?"

The terms "gay and costly" are relative, and take their significance from the connection in which they stand, and the circumstances in which they are applied. There is a sense of propriety in the unperverted mind, which will at once strike the happy medium in any supposed practical case, without resort to an unchangeable and unnecessarily arbitrary and unjust standard. Let it be distinctly understood then, at the outset, that whatever may be said in the following pages, is directed to *the violations of the rule of Christian propriety*, (which rule itself recognizes the *proper distinctions* of rank and position,) and *not* to *infringements of some fancied law of equal restrictions, bringing all to a common level of uniformity.*

The use of "jewelry and gay and costly attire," may be attributed to three causes. 1st. A natural taste for them. 2nd. A desire to gratify others. 3rd. The supposed necessity of compliance with the imperious dictates of Fashion.

In the first case, in so far as the natural emotion itself is concerned, there may be nothing voluntary, and nothing wrong; but when the taste is to be *gratified*, we at once enter the field of *related* voluntary action, and consequent responsibility. The rectitude of the proposed gratification, can not now be determined by the mere fact of a desire for it, or a pleasurable emotion in it. By the great law of inter-influence, the intellect can not be exercised without producing its influence upon the sensibilities and the will. Neither can either of these, without affecting *both the others.* So that any exercise or development of *any* faculty of the mind, *must* produce a corresponding modification of every other faculty. And so interwoven are the mental and moral in man's nature, that whatever affects any part of one, is sure to influence not only its associated parts, but the *whole* of the other. Now with respect to the subject before us, its lawfulness can be determined only by a careful scrutiny of its bearings upon the mental and moral nature. In itself, it is an admiration of jewelry and costly attire, and a desire to enjoy them. Desire always impels toward its object, and if there be no opposing principle, self-love unites in the effort. For the sake of the illustration, we will suppose a colloquy representing the action which each of the mental powers and moral virtues (which are directly interested) may have in the proposed gratification.

Taste. Those adornments are beautiful!

Desire. I must have them.

Self Love. O! they will make me so happy!

Acquisitiveness. But they are very expensive.

Desire. No matter; I must have them—money may as well go in that way as in any other.

Benevolence. The same amount charitably bestowed would do great good.

Pride. Every body else has them, and I am as good as any one.

Sympathy. Widow Needful's suffering babes might be relieved by that amount.

Love. "To him that knoweth to do good, and doeth it not, to him it is sin."

Self Esteem. This *is* doing good. It is making one's self respectable.

Humility. I would not "do evil that good may come."

Approbativeness. Becoming respectable is not doing evil. How can I enjoy Mrs. Vanity's society unless I dress as she does?

Cautiousness. I fear the influence upon others will prove injurious.

Selfishness. Let others take care of themselves. Who 's going to be a saint when all the world are sinners?

Love. I would "do nothing whereby my brother should offend."

Destructiveness. I do n't care; I 'll let Mrs. Flauntout know that I can appear as well as she can!

Veneration. It would seriously interfere with my devotions.

Desire. Give my wishes now—take your devotions afterward.

Reason. It is too degrading to my nature to be tied down to such miserable trash! *I scorn it!*

Self Love. Ah, I see. I should lose more than I would gain by it. No, it must not be.

Selfish Desire. It shall be, let the consequences be as they may.

Conscientiousness. Time misspent, money wasted, influence made destructive, devotion repressed, selfishness stimulated, reason degraded. No, no, it must not be!

Perverse Will. It shall be!!

The experience of every one who has indulged in this practice may not have been in *every respect* as here supposed; but we submit that in every case originating in the cause just named, there are still enough points of resemblance fully to substantiate our conclusion, viz: that it perverts the mental, and does violence to the moral nature, and is intrinsically and unchangeably wrong. *It is self love degenerated into selfishness.* In a great majority of instances, however, the indulgence is not merely for its own sake, but is auxiliary to some other purpose. But whatever that purpose,—whether it be the pleasure it would afford others, or a cringing obedience to Fashion, the essential character of the action is not changed thereby. It still bears the reprobation of Benevolence, Sympathy, Love, Humility, Conscientiousness, Veneration, Reason, Self Love, etc.,—each of which occupies a higher department of our nature than do the mental principles from which this purpose springs, and which must be degraded by it.

We have no right to disturb the balance of our own natures, in order to please the whims, or to respond to the caprices of our fellow men. And when it is done, it is but an exhibition of an inordinate approbativeness, *which is itself sin* when allowed to push us to such extremes, and becomes *Pride* when united with a love for the indulgence itself.

The third cause assigned is, "The imperious dictates of Fashion. But what is this Fashion of which we see and hear so much, and whose potent spell seems to rest in hopeless tyranny upon the race, and yet of which we know so little? It seems to be a general court of appeals in all matters of dress and appearance, whose authority is readily admitted, whose changeful freaks are heartily ridiculed, save by the devoted few who worship most constantly at her shrine, and whose sinful rule is deeply deplored by the good, and vainly reasoned against by the philosophic. But whence comes she, and who gave her the right to rule? It matters not; the right is *questioned* and *denied!* There is not a physiological law of our being, not a law of beauty, and scarcely one of modesty, that has not been violated with impunity, and there is scarcely an imaginable shape of deformity which has not been honored by her smiles and patronage. Well, then, may all the nobler feelings of our nature rise up in indignant reprobation of her claims, and especially in this boasted land of liberty, where civil freedom is the heritage of all, but where this social tyranny binds upon us more ignominious chains than ever kingly despotism dared to rivet. To be compelled to the humiliating confession, that our free-born wives and daughters are daily bowing in the most abject and servile bondage, at the beck of a clique of the most dishonoring specimens of silly humanity that modern civilization has produced, amid the fetid moral atmosphere and polluting associations of Paris, does make our republican blood boil, and forces from us a hearty rebuke of the fawning and cringing degradations. Oh, American women, if you will worship Fashion, at least let it be a thing of your own creating!

Mortifying and disgraceful as it is to our common humanity, and despicable as we feel the slavery to be, we are nevertheless constrained to admit its potency through all ranks of society. Still, there is reason enough left amid the half demented few, and common sense enough yet remaining amid the deluded multitude, to allow one to retain caste (of respectability at least), after daring to enfranchise himself from such ignominious thralldom. The necessity of compliance is, after all, but a *reprehensible moral cowardice*, which finds no justification at the bar of reason, and meets the most indignant rebuke at the hands of insulted and outraged morality; while religion must ever regard it with implacable hostility and insufferable disdain. We need now only to *contrast the nature of this indulgence, as here exhibited, with the* CHARACTER AND WORK OF CHRIST, to prepare us to form a just estimate of his mind concerning it. Of His character, the apostle has given us this brief but expressive portraiture, Heb. vii: 26. "For such a High Priest became us who is *holy, harmless, undefiled, and separate from sinners.*"

And Peter aids our comprehension of its singular loveliness, by declaring, "He did no sin, neither was guile found in his mouth." 1 Peter ii: 22. Nor was this a sinlessness which attracted the attention of his followers only, but the prejudiced and priest-trained multitude exclaimed, "He hath done all things well." Mark vii: 37. And even the devils rendered their homage, in the significant declaration, "I know thee, who thou art, the *Holy One* of God." Mark i: 24.

We can scarcely gaze upon a scene of his

life, or listen to an utterance of his voice, that does not tell us of some exalted virtue, or shadow forth the workings of his heart of love. "I seek not mine own glory." John viii: 50. "Take my yoke upon you and learn of me, for I am *meek and lowly* in heart." Matt. xi: 29. These are the affirmations of a humility as profound as it was natural, and as natural as it was rare. His night-long prayers (Luke vi: 12), upon the lone mountain, secluded from the bustle of the world which he came to redeem, attested his devotion; while his evening journeys from Jerusalem to Bethany told how he felt the attachments of friendship's home, and his flowing tears before the tomb of Lazarus, proclaimed the tender sympathies of his nature—sympathies which were but faintly echoed in the wondering exclamation of the Jewish kindred, "Behold how he loved him!" The garden witnessed his peaceful resignation when it listened to the trembling accents which a supernatural agony wrung from his fainting spirit, "O my Father, if it be possible, let this cup pass from me; nevertheless, not as I will, but as thou wilt." Matt. xxvi: 39. His magnanimous and forgiving disposition was heard in the God-like tones which fell from the cross of Calvary, "Father, forgive them, for they know not what they do."

Thus the character of Christ, in all its unique and majestic bearing, stands before us, *alone!* He was man, for he walked among men as one of their kind, yet how infinitely above man. He had no prototype—no fellow—no successor. Isolated in its solemn grandeur, that character stands, the admiration of the world. Other men had possessed the virtues of humanity to no small degree. Job was patient, Moses was meek, Abraham was faithful, David was devoted, Solomon was wise, but Christ was *all in one.* He was patience, meekness, faith, love, devotion, wisdom, all *personified.* He was every thing good that moralist, poet, or theologian ever wrote, and if there be any nameless excellence which thought has never compassed, or language lisped, He was that excellence too, living, breathing, acting, an outstanding *fact* for men to imitate and angels love. How pure, how elevated, how transcendently lovely, was such a character! The innocence of the smiling babe, the love of the self-forgetful mother, the philanthropy of a Howard, the patriotism of a Washington, the self-sacrificing zeal of the missionary martyr, all these appeal to the soul with resistless power.. We could not if we would withhold from them the spontaneous admiration of our heaven-taught hearts. How much less can we refrain from rendering the suffrage of our souls to Him who was all this and *more.* Yea, more than pen can tell. And His work, how grand! To be the High Priest of a nation was a coveted station. The High Priest of the world was he! The rescue of a fatherland from the fetters of bondage, shall insure a historic name, and a fame as wide as the love of noble deeds and daring. He redeemed a world. Look now upon that character. Is there any thing in it sordid, base, or unholy?

When he might have commanded wealth and fared sumptuously every day, hear his mournful plaint. "Foxes have holes, and birds of the air *have* nests, but the son of man hath not where to lay *his* head." (Luke, ix: 58.) Is there any thing here calculated to engender pride, or excite vanity? Do you detect any attempt at display, or any encouragement of extravagance? Had there been, would not his inveterate foes have urged that sin against him? But hark. "The chief priest, and elders, and all the council, sought false witness against Jesus to put him to death, but found none." (Matt., xxvi: 59, 60.) No, not even false witness, such had been the immaculate purity of his life. And even the reckless and perjured Pilate was compelled to exclaim before the persecuting priests, "I find no fault in this man," (Luke, xxiii: 4,) and finally washed his hands and said, "I am innocent of the blood of this just person, see ye *to it.*" (Matt., xxvii: 24.)

Now let us turn to the contemplation of his work.

He came to establish a kingdom which he declares "is not of this world," (John, xviii: 36,) and which was announced to Mary as an everlasting kingdom, (Luke, i: 32, 33,) the principles of which are "righteousness and judgment," (Isa., xxxii: 1,) which is to be ordered and established with "judgment and justice from henceforth even for ever." (Isa., ix: 7.)

Over this kingdom he reigns. He taught its laws of admission and enjoyment. "Except ye repent ye shall all likewise perish." (Luke, xiii: 3.) "The Father loveth the Son and hath given all things into his hand. He that believeth on the Son hath everlasting life; and he that believeth not the Son, shall not see life; but the wrath of God abideth on him." (John, iii: 35, 36.) Such are the laws of admission —Repentance and Faith. What are those of enjoyment? A certain lawyer asked the Savior, "Master, which *is* the great commandment in the law? Jesus said unto him, Thou shalt love the Lord thy God with all thy heart, and with all thy soul, and with all thy mind. This is the first and great commandment. And the second *is* like unto it, Thou shalt love thy neighbor as thyself. On these two commandments hang all the law and the prophets." (Matt., xxii: 36-40.) The Gospel, too, has its commandment; the one great law which meets us at the very threshold, with an exclusiveness as utter and decided as the eternal relations of the redeemed to the Redeemer can make it. "*Ye are not your own, for ye are bought with a price: therefore glorify God in your body, and in your spirit, which are God's.*" (1 Cor., vi: 19, 20.) This is the one eternal, inviolable, and unchangeable law which stands as the basis of all others. Every other law in the New Testament is but a *statute* regulating the observance of this grand enactment in particular respects. What, then, does this law mean?

Certainly *all that each separate precept or statute specifies*, and as *much more*, (if more be possible,) as may lie within the range of human ability to do, to glorify God. His work then, was to *teach* this law in all its varied applications, to exemplify his commands by the practical purity of his life, and by tireless industry, and unflagging zeal and devotion to the great work of saving the world, to exhibit to that world at once the yearnings of infinite compassion and the example which his people were to follow. Hence says the Apostle (1 Peter, ii: 21.) "For even hereunto were ye called: because Christ also suffered for us, leaving us an example, that ye should follow his steps." He established his kingdom, and left us a record of the work and of its laws, in the Gospels and Epistles, and now we may search these through and through, and we shall find all in perfect keeping with his character. The purity, meekness, and loveliness of his character shine through his work. In vain we look for any thing which can be pleaded as an authorization of worldly conformity, or for any principle which, in its legitimate course of action, can develop the unlovely and depraved passions of human nature.

On the contrary, there seems a studied reserve, nay, rather a bold and decided position of antagonism to the world, in its fashions, maxims, and policy. While the world is naturally and essentially selfish, grasping, and proud, here is naught but humility, self-sacrifice, a noble consecration of time, means, and energies to the good of all, a purity which "avoids the appearance of evil," and a heavenly mindedness which constantly declares that we are but strangers and pilgrims here, and that we "seek a city whose builder and maker is God."

The proof adduced by this contrast needs not to be sought for; it forces itself upon us with all the authority of a perfect moral demonstration. That which is *born* of the world, *nourished* by the world, *lives for* the world, and *wears the livery* of the world, must be in changeless hostility to Christ. "Can two walk together except they be agreed?" "*Ye can not serve God and Mammon.*"

We infer the mind of Christ, in the second place:

From the general scope and spirit of scripture, and its statements in analogous cases. It is an established rule of interpretation, that particular passages of any book must be construed in harmony with the general spirit of the work. Especially is this rule applicable in scripture criticism, since the work of a perfect being must necessarily harmonize in all its parts.

Nor are we in this case left to gather a knowledge of its design and spirit from a careful survey of the whole production, since we have, in a few plain declarations, the *summary* of the inspired penmen themselves. "For whatsoever things were written aforetime, were written for our learning, that we, through patience and comfort of the scriptures, might have hope." (Rom., xv : 4.) "Wherefore lay apart all filthiness and superfluity of naughtiness, and receive with meekness the engrafted word, which is able to save your souls." (James, i: 21.) "So then faith *cometh* by hearing, and hearing by the word of God." (Rom., x: 17.) "But these are written, that ye might believe that Jesus is the Christ, the Son of God; and that believing, ye might have life through his name." (John, xx: 31.) "And these things write we unto you, that your joy may be full." (1 John, i: 4.) "And that from a child thou hast known the holy scriptures, which are able to make thee wise unto salvation through faith which is in Christ Jesus. All scripture *is* given by inspiration of God, and *is* profitable for doctrine, for reproof, for correction, for instruction in righteousness; that the man of God may be perfect, thoroughly furnished unto all good works." (2 Tim., iii: 15–17.)

The aim of the scriptures then, is that we "may have hope;" that we may "lay apart all filthiness and superfluity of naughtiness, and receive with meekness the engrafted word;" that we may save our souls through the faith that "cometh by hearing;" that "believing we might have life through his name;" that our "joy may be full;" that we may be led to the adoption of the pure and self-denying "doctrines" of Christ; to "reprove" in us all worldly conformity and sinful habits; to "correct" all errors of the life which result from wrong views of saving truth; and so "to instruct in righteousness" as to secure the abandonment of all unholy practices, and the attainment of the perfection which consists in being "thoroughly furnished unto all good works."

The word "thoroughly" means *perfectly;* perfectly prepared for all good works. No comment of ours can possibly place this in a stronger light than does the Apostle himself. We have seen, in our preliminary examination of the nature of the gratification which we condemn, that it springs from selfishness and pride, or undue deference to the wishes of others, or a sinful moral cowardice which dare not resist the mandates of Fashion.

Most conclusively may we now press the inquiries, "Can the evil tree bear good fruit?" or will the "bitter fountain send forth sweet waters?" Are those persons who are in the daily exercise of such dispositions, and thus by the inevitable law of habit *intensifying* them, are they perfectly prepared for self-abandonment, and entire separation from the world, and "thoroughly furnished *unto all good works?*" Can they respond, as they otherwise might, to the calls of benevolence, while adorning themselves with the price of souls? And can there be any doubt concerning the mind of Christ in reference to these things? If so, the particular passages which we shall soon quote, must put that doubt to rest for ever; for certainly, *these*, if not the *scope* of the Bible, will indicate its author's mind.

We go, then, to the definite statements of Scripture in analogous cases.

Those cases may be deemed analogous which originate in similar causes, exhibit like dispositions, or produce similar results. The analogy too, may often be inferred by a *prohibition* of particular sins, or by the inculcation of opposite virtues. With this fact in mind, it will at once be perceived that our proposition covers almost the entire ground of scripture precept and inhibition.

We shall confine our examples, however, to a few of the most common. The evil and danger of selfishness, and the duty of self-denial, are strongly and frequently insisted upon by the sacred writers. "Whosoever will come after me, let him deny himself, and take up his cross, and follow me." (Mark, viii: 34.) "He that hath two coats, let him impart to him that hath none; and he that hath meat, let him do likewise." (Luke, iii: 11.) "Ye have heard that it hath been said, An eye for an eye, and a tooth for a tooth: but I say unto you, That ye resist not evil: but whosoever shall smite thee on thy right cheek, turn to him the other also. And if any man will sue thee at the law, and take away thy coat, let him have *thy* cloak also. And whosoever shall compel thee to go a mile, go with him twain. Give to him that asketh thee, and from him that would borrow of thee, turn not thou away." (Matt., v: 38-41.) "Then Jesus beholding him, loved him, and said unto him, One thing thou lackest: go thy way, sell whatsoever thou hast, and give to the poor, and thou shalt have treasure in heaven: and come, take up the cross, and follow me. And he was sad at that saying, and went away grieved: for he had great possessions." (Mark, x: 21, 22.) "So likewise, whosoever he be of you that forsaketh not all that he hath, he cannot be my disciple." (Luke, xiv: 33.) "I beseech you therefore, brethren, by the mercies of God, that ye present your bodies a living sacrifice, holy, acceptable unto God, *which is* your reasonable service." (Rom., xii: 1.) "Hereby perceive we the love *of God*, because he laid down his life for us: and we ought to lay down *our* lives for the brethren." (1 John, iii: 16.)

Against the *cares of the world*, producing their stinting and disastrous effects, we are faithfully warned by our Savior in the parable of the sower. "He also that received seed among the thorns, is he that heareth the word;

and the care of this world, and the deceitfulness of riches, choke the word, and he becometh unfruitful." (Matt., xiii: 22.)

And the Apostle James cautions us against any *omissions of duty*, or *neglect of the opportunities of doing good* which Providence opens before us. "Therefore to him that knoweth to do good, and doeth *it* not, to him it is sin." (James, iv: 17.) "As we have therefore opportunity, let us do good unto all *men*, especially unto those who are of the household of faith." (Gal., vi: 10.)

Our responsibility for the *proper improvement of all our talents*, is made the subject of two of the most impressive parables ever uttered by the Savior. "Then shall the kingdom of heaven be likened unto ten virgins, which took their lamps," etc. (Matt., xxv: 1-13.) "For *the kingdom of heaven is* as a man traveling into a far country, *who* called his own servants," etc. (Matt., xxv: 14-30.) "But he that knew not, and did commit things worthy of stripes, shall be beaten with few *stripes*. For unto whomsoever much is given, of him shall be much required: and to whom men have committed much, of him they will ask the more." (Luke, xii: 48.)

All *worldly mindedness* is condemned in unsparing language, and the scriptures seem solicitous to guard against its remotest approach, by sounding repeated notes of warning and reproof. "And be not conformed to this world; but be ye transformed by the renewing of your mind, that ye may prove what *is* that good, and acceptable, and perfect, will of God." (Rom., xii: 2.) "Set your affections on things above, not on things on the earth." (Col., iii: 2.) "Love not the world, neither the things *that are* in the world. If any man love the world, the love of the Father is not in him." (1 John, ii: 15.) "Know ye not that the friendship of the world is enmity with God? . Whosoever, therefore, will be a friend of the world is the enemy of God." (James, iv: 4.) "Wherefore come out from among them, and be ye separate, saith the Lord, and touch not the unclean *thing;* and I will receive you." (2 Cor., vi: 17.)

Lest the purity of the christian church should be compromised with evil, we are commanded to avoid "the appearance of evil." (1 Thess., v: 22.) "Enter not into the path of the wicked, and go not in the way of evil *men.* Avoid it, pass not by it, turn from it, and pass away." (Prov., iv: 14, 15.) "I have not sat with vain persons, neither will I go in with dissemblers." (Psa., xxvi: 4.) "Be not ye therefore partakers with them. For ye were some time darkness, but now *are ye* light in the Lord: walk as children of light; (for the fruit of the spirit *is* in all goodness, righteousness and truth;) proving what is acceptable unto the Lord. And have no fellowship with the unfruitful works of darkness, but rather reprove *them*." (Eph., v: 7-11.)

If we may not have even the external appearance of evil, much less may we *seduce to evil*. "Neither shalt thou make marriages with them; thy daughter thou shalt not give unto his son, nor his daughter shalt thou take unto thy son. For they will turn away thy son from following me, that they may serve other gods: so will the anger of the Lord be kindled against you, and destroy thee suddenly. But thus shall ye deal with them; ye shall destroy their altars, and break down their images, and cut down their groves, and burn their graven images with fire." "The graven images of their gods shall ye burn with fire: thou shalt not desire the silver or gold *that is* on them, nor take *it* unto thee, lest thou be snared therein: for it *is* an abomination to the Lord, thy God. Neither shalt thou bring an abomination into thy house, lest thou be a cursed thing like it; *but* thou shalt utterly detest it, and thou shalt utterly abhor it; for it *is* a cursed thing." (Deut., vii: 3, 4, 5, 25, 26.) "Ye shall utterly destroy all the places wherein the nations which ye shall possess, served their gods, upon the high mountains, and upon the hills, and under every green tree. And ye shall overthrow their altars, and break their pillars, and burn their groves with fire; and ye shall hew down the graven images of their gods, and destroy the names of them out of that place. Ye shall not do so unto the Lord, your God." "When the Lord thy God shall cut off the nations from before thee, whither thou goest to possess them, and thou succeedest them, and dwellest in their land; take heed to thyself that thou be not snared by following them, after that they be destroyed from before thee; and that thou inquire not after their gods, saying, How did these nations serve their gods? even so will I do likewise. Thou shalt not do so unto the Lord thy God: for every abomination to the Lord which he hateth, have they done unto their gods; for even their sons and their daughters they have burnt in the fire to their gods." (Deut., xii: 2-4, 29-31.) "But whoso shall offend one of these little ones which believe in me, it were better for him that a millstone were hanged about his neck, and *that* he were drowned in the depth of the sea." (Matt., xviii: 6.)

Pride and haughtiness are thus spoken of by the Prophet and the New Testament writers. "Moreover the Lord saith, Because the daughters of Zion are haughty, and walk with stretched forth necks and wanton eyes, walking and mincing *as* they go, and making a tinkling with their feet: therefore, the Lord will smite with a scab the crown of the head of the daughters of Zion, and the Lord will discover their secret parts. In that day the Lord will take away the bravery of *their* tinkling ornaments *about their feet,* and *their* cauls and *their* round tires like the moon, the chains, and the bracelets, and the mufflers, the bonnets, and the ornaments of the legs, and the headbands, and the tablets, and the ear-rings, the rings, and nose jewels, the changeable suits of apparel, and the mantles, and the wimples, and the crisping pins, the glasses, and the fine linen, and the hoods, and the vails. And it shall come to pass, *that* instead of sweet smell there shall be stink; and instead of a girdle, a rent; and instead of well set hair, baldness; and instead of a stomacher, a girding of sackcloth; *and* burning instead of beauty." (Isaiah, iii: 16–24.) "How can ye believe, which receive honor one of an other, and seek not the honor that *cometh* from God only?" (John, v: 44.) "Beware lest any man spoil you through philosophy and vain deceit, after the tradition of men, after the rudiments of the world, and not after Christ." (Col., ii: 8.) "My brethren, have not the faith of our Lord Jesus Christ, *the Lord* of glory, with respect of persons. For if there come unto your assembly a man with a gold ring, in goodly apparel, and there come in also a poor man in vile raiment; and ye have respect to him that weareth the gay clothing, and say unto him, Sit thou here in a good place; and say to the poor, Stand thou there, or sit here under my footstool; are ye not then partial in yourselves, and are become judges of evil thoughts?" (James, ii: 1–4.) "Then spake Jesus to the multitude and to his disciples, saying, The Scribes and the Pharisees sit in Moses' seat: all therefore whatsoever they bid you observe, *that* observe and do; but do not ye after their works: for they say and do not. For they bind heavy burdens and grievous to be borne, and lay *them* on men's shoulders; but they *themselves* will not move them with one of their fingers. But all their works they do for to be seen of men; they make broad their phylacteries, and enlarge the borders of their garments, and love the uppermost rooms at feasts, and the chief seats in the synagogues, and greetings in the markets, and to be called of men, Rabbi, Rabbi. But be not ye called Rabbi; for one is your master, *even* Christ; and all ye are brethren." (Matt., xxiii: 1–8.)

It will not be necessary to quote the numerous precepts inculcating the opposite virtues, as they will at once recur to every reader of the sacred volume.

We now have the argument from analogy fairly before us.

Whenever any action springs from like causes, exhibits like principles, or is attended with similar results to those mentioned in the quotations above, it meets the ban of Jehovah in reiterated passages of his word. So uniform is this that no one can doubt that it is because of a fundamental antagonism with the principles and purposes of his government; and that whatever course of human conduct may be justly charged with the same character, must expect the same condemnation. In regard to the subject before us, the conclusion is so plain that it can be controverted only by a denial of the argument previously stated concerning the nature of the indulgence. But for the present we shall assume the validity of that, as the progress of the discussion will bring corroborating testimony enough to place it upon the immovable basis of demonstration so clear that none but the perversely obstinate can fail to perceive its force.

An other method of ascertaining the mind of Christ relative to this matter has been already anticipated in the progress of the argument. It is—

From the effect of such adornment upon Christian character. Says one, "I never yet found pride in a noble nature, nor humility in an unworthy mind. Of all trees, I observe that God hath chosen the vine, a low plant that creeps helpless upon a wall; of all beasts, the soft and patient lamb; of all fowls, the mild and guileless dove. When God appeared to Moses, it was not in a lofty cedar, nor in the sturdy oak, nor the spreading palm, but a bush, an humble, slender, abject bush; as if he would, by these selections, check the arrogance of man. Nothing procureth love like humility; nothing hate, like pride."

We may add, that we have never seen the habit of adornment which was not associated with pride, usually in the ratio of its own extent.

A lady once asked a clergyman "Whether he considered such a practice as an evidence of pride?" He replied, with as much philosophy as point: "Madam, when you see the fox's tail peeping out of the hole, you may be sure that he is within." It is at least a singular coincidence which demands explanation at the hands of objectors, that the most vain, conceited, and silly, are uniformly the persons most addicted to the habit, while the most staid, sober, and truly refined are the least prone to its exhibition.

And most unfortunately for any explanation that might be offered, the great law of inter-influence asserts a connection between the outward appearance and the inner gauge by which that appearance is regulated. And the Apostle, as if in recognition of this truth, more than intimated a hopelessness of witnessing "*the ornament* of a meek and quiet spirit" conjoined with the "*adorning* of plaiting of the hair, and of wearing of gold, or of putting on of apparel." Those most addicted to the last named habit, are notoriously the least reliable in all the self-sacrificing duties of christianity. Though some will attribute their want of consistency to other causes, we can not accept the explanation until they tell us why it is that these "other causes" are so inseparable from this practice; and even if they succeed in this, the fact still remains that this indulgence is found in very dangerous company. It is matter of extreme doubt which is worshiped the more by our most fashionable professors, the God of the sanctuary, or "the beauty of a hat;" which is thought of the more, the sermon, or the most advantageous way to display the last "splendid silk;" which is remembered the longer, the practical instructions of the sacred desk, or the want of taste exhibited in some rival's adornments; which is desired the more, religious profit, or an opportunity to "create a sensation." Not that we charge *all* this directly upon the adornments of the individual, but we do impeach them as guilty of *strengthening the mental tastes which demand them*, and as *originating those tastes in others and perpetuating them to the exclusion of better ones, every where within the circle of their influence.*

"A minister in the city of New York was, a few years since, called in to visit a dying young lady, about twenty years of age, who was heiress to a large estate, whose parents were dotingly fond of her, and whose education had been of the highest and most fashionable character. The minister talked of death, judgment, and eternity; but the young lady had never before heard such language addressed to her, and she trembled. In the dying hour she called for some of her fine clothes; and when they were brought, she looked at her mother, and said, 'These have ruined me. You never told me I must die. You taught me that my errand in this world was to be gay and dressy, and to enjoy the vanities of life. What could you mean? You knew I must die, and go to judgment. You never told me to read the Bible, or to go to church, unless to make a display of some new finery. Mother, you have ruined me.' She died in a few moments after."

In the sad instance here narrated, it would be difficult, and perhaps undesirable to determine the precise amount of blame-worthiness to be attached to the mother's passion for display, a passion so intense and blinding, that it voluntarily periled the immortal interests of her child; but none can fail to perceive the destructive tendency of any principle when permitted to develop itself in the *Christian's bosom*, which has *proved how ruinous it is* in the character of the *unregenerate*. That the last play, or the opera, or the cotillion party, or the levee, or the fashions, should form the substance of the conversation and the thoughts of the professed followers of Christ, would seem too much to be believed, did not their outward adornments indicate the mental principles which control them. The passion, naturally strong enough, has been strengthened by indulgence, till it sways the mind with a species of intoxicating power almost perfect in its control. But the injury does not consist altogether in the development of this part of the nature; for the indulgencies themselves have unforseen connections with others and these with still others, *till the entire round of worldly pleasure becomes complicated in the first gratification*, and the conscience, deliberately stained in the first instance, loses every firm ground of support for resistance in each succeeding allurement, till both the power and the inclination to resist the evil are well nigh spent, and the Holy Spirit is grieved away, and barrenness and leanness fill the soul. "The tendency of any thing may be best understood, by considering an extreme case as an illustration. Dress up a little girl for the first time in fine attire, and adorn her with all the ornaments of our grown up daughters, and you will have a specimen of the ridiculous pomposity of childish vanity. But why are the affected strut and fulsome airs so ridiculous? Simply because it is native vanity acting itself out, without the restraints which social life throws around those of more mature years. But in either case, the vanity is *there*, as the endless twists, and turns, and adjustments which the mirror of the dressing chamber beholds, can testify. As truly as indulgence feeds desire, does this practice increase the native vanity which prompted to it." (Gift of Power, page 253.)

It is said that Louis Fifteenth, of France, in order to make a public procession in Paris the most gorgeous that ever was witnessed in that luxurious city, had a little child covered with gold leaf, and carried in splendid state before the people. The graceful movements of the little golden god excited immense applause; but before the train had marched its appointed course, he was seized with a sudden trembling and fell down *dead.* The impervious metal had stopped the pores of his skin, and he was suffocated amid the joyous acclamations that his appearance elicited. Alas! how many there are, who, like this victim of ambitious pride, shine in all the dazzling splendors which riches and fashion can throw around them, and who, like him, are being suffocated spiritually, inch by inch, in the midst of their coveted triumphs.

"Whoso readeth let him understand."

Another method of learning the mind of Christ, is by his deputy, the Holy Spirit.

When the Savior left the world, he promised to his disciples "another comforter," who should lead them into "all truth," and should remain as his agent in the affairs of His kingdom, until He should come the second time, to reign "over all, God blessed for ever." This comforter, the Holy Spirit, was given upon the day of Pentecost in a peculiar manner, and from that time became the acknowledged guide of the church. His promptings upon the Christian heart, if satisfactorily ascertained, may always be received as an infallible rule in all things relating to either faith or practice. The question now is, What are the Holy Spirit's promptings relative to the indulgence before us? In the fact that the mind of the Spirit has been already recorded in the Bible upon this very point, we have more than a presumption what his suggestion will be. Besides, it gives peculiar significance to a truth which we must premise in this connection, viz: that the *absence* of such promptings in some cases, or even in a majority of instances, is not to be considered as favoring the view that He is indifferent to the subject. For such is the training of youth, that they are taught to believe in the rightfulness and even the necessity of such indulgences, so that the avenue to conviction is not only closed, but barred by the habits of a lifetime, and the example of church members everywhere. On the contrary, the *least intimation* from the Spirit in the face of all this training and its consequences, should be regarded as a most serious thing. For the Spirit never does any thing without a necessity for it, while it is often prevented from acting, by the obstacles which corrupt human nature has placed in its pathway. This being the case, whenever in the experience of any one, while the heart is tender and ready to obey every behest of the Spirit, some suggestions toward the abandonment of a previous habit of adornment are made, even though those suggestions be no more than mere questions of doubtfulness concerning the rightfulness or expediency of the custom, and even though those questions assume only the fragmentary character of a *passing thought*, without even the distinct outline of a well-defined inquiry, with *all these limitations* they should be regarded as very strong indications of the mind of Christ. If in addition to this, the voice of the Spirit is often heard in the hours of first love, or heard until it meets a *distinct denial*, kindly remonstrating, or lovingly rebuking the practice, there is then no room for mistake. But if even further than all this, He peremptorily demands renunciation of the indulgence, or a guilty conscience as the only alternative, the issue is distinctly taken, and it then becomes those who controvert the position here assumed, to show cause why they should be denied the indulgence, if it be so innocent in itself as the objector affirms.

"Miss T——, of ——county, who was very thoughtless, was induced by a friend to promise that she would read the "Rise and Progress." Her feelings followed those of the writer generally, and with as little opposition as could be expected until she came to the 17th chapter. That is styled the "self-dedication chapter." While transcribing this chapter, according to the author's direction, to make it her own act, consecrating herself to Jehovah's service, for time and for ever, she hesitated. Her wicked heart arose in opposition. She could not surrender *all* to God. There was a *small portion* of her earthly treasures, a little *shining dust*, used as ornaments of her perishing body, which she was unwilling to surrender for that "glittering crown of glory," which Christ promises to all those that love and serve him. In great agony her pen was laid aside, and for several days she refused to finish the dedication chapter. One day, while complaining to a sister (since gone to rest) that she could find no peace, her sister replied, "Perhaps there is something you are unwilling to part with, some *little* thing that you will not give up for the sake of an interest in Christ? Remember he requires *entire* consecration, *all*." She soon left her sister, retired to her closet, resolved to part with her jewelry and all things else for an interest in her Redeemer. She was immediately able to finish transcribing her chapter, light began to dawn upon her soul, and her proud spirit was humbled. Peace gradually dawned upon her mind, and as soon as an opportunity presented she united with the church, and now walks in newness of life."

Such instances are not rare in the observation of those who are called to direct seeking souls to the Redeemer, and each one proclaims in trumpet-tones against the indulgence.

We may now appeal directly to christian experience.

It is a fact that in *all* evangelical churches there are more or fewer, who are taught by the Spirit to refrain from such gratifications, and we submit, that as a general rule, in all churches the most holy and useful persons systematically and conscientiously stand aloof from such practices.

The mere fact that those who enjoy the most intimate communion with the Father and the Son do refrain from such indulgences, is a powerful argument either for the essential wrongfulness or inexpediency of them.

But it would be easy to show that the inexpedient in religious matters is necessarily wrong; therefore, the conduct of the holy, viewed in the light of their divinely received instructions, pronounces authoritatively the anathema of Heaven upon the sin. Another fact in clear connection with the foregoing is, that persons of no marked piety, but whose experience is changeable, not unfrequently feel strong scruples and sometimes keen remorse of conscience for their habits of adornment, *especially in seasons of revival*, or of *unusual personal interest in religious concerns*. Though the feeling dies away with relapsing piety, it is revived again with the fresh springing of religious joys.

The rational conclusion from the above is that the Spirit speaks *as clearly* and as unambiguously as *the false education* and *perverted practices* of the church will allow, especially when all this is wilfully done after the decisive utterances of Holy Writ, and in direct contravention of its authority.

Let us here pause and survey the ground. The character and work of Christ have been exhibited first, in order that the weight of their testimony might not only bear upon the general argument, but prevent the cavils which might otherwise be urged against the succeeding propositions. The scope and spirit of scripture and its statements in analogous cases, thus not only preserve their inherent weight, but have a cumulative power from the character and work of Christ. The effects of the indulgence upon Christian character, then, shows the line of its divergence from Christ and from sacred truth, ever widening as it passes through practical experience, while the voice of the Holy Spirit, in unison with Christ, as a summary of truth, and a guardian of christian graces, constantly sounds its notes of warning and reproof.

Here we might safely rest our plea, but all the foregoing has but prepared the way for another witness, whose testimony is utterly unimpeachable, and at this stage of the proceedings, equally unmistakeable. Then "to the Law and the Testimony."

There are express and positive statements of scripture upon the point. In 1 Peter, iii: 3, 4, we have these words: "Whose adorning, let it not be that outward *adorning* of plaiting the hair, and of wearing of gold, or of putting on of apparel; but *let it be* the hidden man of the heart, in that which is not corruptible, *even the ornament* of a meek and quiet spirit, which is, in the sight of God, of great price."

"To show there is no possibility of evading the force of these commands, and that they are binding upon all who profess the religion of Christ, and that he who tramples upon them does it at his peril, let us inquire, What degree of respect should we render to the express prohibitions of scripture, and how far may we qualify them in our interpretations? In regard to the first part of the inquiry, it is evident that a prohibition, emanating from the same source, and attended with the same sanctions, is equally as authoritative as an express command. The Decalogue itself places this beyond question, for eight of the ten commandments are in the form of prohibitions.

"As to the interpretation which we are to give to such words as those of Peter, a high authority has said: 'I hold it for a most infallible rule in expositions of sacred scripture that when a literal construction will stand, the furthest from the letter is commonly the worst. There is nothing more dangerous than this licentious and deluding art, which changeth the meaning of words, as alchemy doth, or would do, the substance of metals; maketh of every thing what it listeth, and bringeth in the end all truth to nothing.'—See Hooker's Eccl. Polity, book 5, chap. 59.

"Dr. Peck, before quoting the above, says: 'Language is always to be understood in its natural or literal sense, unless there is something in the nature of the subject to which it is applied which requires the restricted meaning.' Applying this rule to the subject before us, we conclude that the passage from Peter, with which we commenced signifies only what the words, used in their plain, natural, and obvious meaning, convey, and contains *all that meaning* without evasion or limitation. To this it may be objected, 'that it was undoubtedly intended to be understood thus, at the time when it was written, but was not designed to be of perpetual obligation.'

"In reply, we may state another rule of interpretation. (See Horner's Introduction, abridged, p. 152.) 'Negatives are *binding at all times;* that is, we must never do that which is forbidden, though good may ultimately come from it.'

"Another consideration which shows this passage to be of general application, is, that it was first written by Peter, to all Christians, and, that about four or five years afterward, it was deemed of sufficient importance to form a part of Paul's instructions to Timothy, as pastor of the church at Ephesus: 'In like manner also, that women adorn themselves in modest apparel, with shamefacedness and sobriety; not with braided hair, or gold, or pearls, or costly array; but (which becometh women professing godliness) with good works.' (1 Tim. ii. 9, 10.) This gave it a fresh sanction, and rendered it obligatory upon the ministry to enforce the rule given for the government of all.

"Besides, the same reasons exist for it now as then. In confirmation of all the above, it may be well to consider the fact that no such moral text ever has but one meaning; which meaning is to be ascertained just as we would that of any other writing, viz: by the whole scope of the context, taken in connection with the general sentiments of the writer. The scope is here plainly announced, by saying that the purpose is to win the husband. (See 1 Peter, iii: 1.) That this may be done, husbands must see their wives observing a 'chaste conversation, coupled with fear,' and keeping the command already mentioned, 'whose adorning let it not be that outward *adorning* of plaiting the hair, and of wearing of gold, or of putting on of apparel; but *let it be* the hidden man of the heart, in that which is not corruptible, *even the ornament of* a meek and quiet spirit. which is, in the sight of God, of great price.' 'For after this manner, in the old time the holy women also, who trusted in God, adorned themselves,' etc. Let common sense say which would be the most likely to win the husband or others from the world to Christ, the exhibition of the spirit of vanity, which loves to be decked in the gaudy trappings of the world, or the meek and quiet spirit, which is, in the sight of God, of great price. The general sentiments of the writer, none can deny, favor a total separation from the world, in spirit and in practice.

"It would be needless to quote passages in illustration of the fact. (See chap. i: 13, 14; chap. ii: 9, 12; chap. iv: 1, 3, etc.) We conclude, then, that if there is any meaning at all in those passages, *it is that which is borne out upon the very face of the words employed, and that we have no right to bend them to any other.*

"By what authority can any one expunge this commandment from the sacred oracles, or, what is equivalent to it, explain away its force, and make it a mere form of words, with no meaning and no sanction? Let such beware, lest he practically bring upon himself the curse denounced against such as 'take away from the words of the book,' etc. (Rev. xxii: 19.)" (Gift of Power, pp. 270–272.)

But as such passages are practically considered of so little significance, an analytical view of them may better enable us to apprehend their meaning.

1 Tim., ii: 9, 10.	1 Peter, iii: 3, 4.
"In like manner also, that women adorn themselves, . . .	"Whose adorning,
not with braided hair, or gold, or pearls, or costly array, . . .	let it not be that outward *adorning* of plaiting the hair, and of wearing of gold, or of putting on of apparel;
but . . . in modest apparel,	but *let it be* the hidden man

with shame-facedness and sobriety," and "(which becometh women professing godliness) with good works."	of the heart in that which is not corruptible, *even the ornament* of a meek and quiet spirit, which is in the sight of God of great price."

The collation of these parallel passages shows that there are two kinds of adornment permitted, ("modest apparel" and "good works,") and one forbidden. "*Whose adorning*," *i.e.*, the adornment of the *necessary apparel*, (for the "modest apparel," when attended with the "meek and quiet spirit" and good works which "*becometh*" them and is of "great price before God,") *is one ornament*, but is opposed to an other "outward adornment," which consists in "braided hair, and gold, and pearls, and costly array," which last is supposed to be inconsistent with the "hidden man of the heart," "the meek and quiet spirit," etc., which is the second adornment permitted.

The meaning of the Apostles is well conveyed in a liberal rendering with which we have been favored by James Strong, S. T. D. (1 Peter, iii: 3, 4.) "Of whom let there be not the outward ornament of imbraiding of hair and investiture of golden (trinkets,) or putting on of garments, but the concealed man of the heart, in the incorrupt (state) of the mild and quiet spirit which is high-priced before God."

1 Tim., ii: 9, 10. "Likewise, also, (I will) that the women adorn themselves in decorous habiliments, with modesty and sobriety, not in braids, or gold, or pearls, or high-priced clothing, but (which becomes women promising piety,) through good works."

The opposition between the different members of the sentences embraced, prove conclusively that the apostle meant to be understood as teaching the *essential incongruity* of the outward ornaments, and the "*incorrupt (state) of the mild and quiet spirit which is high-priced before God.*"

Thus agree Clarke, Wesley, Benson, Robinson, Conybeare, Burkitt, Olshausen, Scott, Barnes, etc.

The truth is, there is no possibility of evading the plain, literal construction of these inspired words. And if inspired, they *mean* some thing. Reader, pause and learn that meaning before you dare to trifle further with their prohibited indulgences. Nor deem them trifles. God's book is not made up of trifles. And if it were, the practice which they reprove can not be a trifle, so long as it is loved so well that you refuse to surrender it in obedience to a divine command.

If any thing more were needed to demonstrate absolutely the truth of the above position, it is found in the corroborating passages which abound throughout the Bible.

"I have given them thy word; and the world hath hated them, because they are not of the world, even as I am not of the world. I pray not that thou shouldst take them out of the world, but that thou shouldst keep them from the evil. They are not of the world, even as I am not of the world." (John, xvii: 14–16.)

"Love not the world, neither the things *that are* in the world. If any man love the world, the love of the Father is not in him." (1 John, ii: 15.)

"Ye adulterers and adulteresses, know ye not that the friendship of the world is enmity with God? whosoever therefore will be a friend of the world is the enemy of God." (James, iv: 4.)

"I beseech you therefore, brethren, by the mercies of God, that ye present your bodies a living sacrifice, holy, acceptable unto God, *which is* your reasonable service. And be not conformed to this world, but be ye transformed by the renewing of your mind, that ye may prove what *is* that good, and acceptable, and perfect will of God." (Rom., xii: 1, 2.)

If these are not sufficiently decisive, we not only despair of finding any thing in the scriptures that would be, but we renounce the hope that language can furnish terms sufficiently explicit and strong to settle the question. Nor can it. For so perverting is the indulgence, that the love of it will impel many to quibble where every thing is plain, object where every thing is reasonable, torture to false meanings from hatred to the true, deny what is clearly demonstrated, and persist in their course, braving all consequences.

We have now answered the question, "What is the mind of Christ with respect to Christians adorning their persons with jewelry and gay and costly attire," in six distinct particulars, each of which contains evidence enough to convince any jury in the land, in any case of civil jurisprudence; and all of which united, forms a body of testimony which is utterly irresistible, except by those whose willful blindness would afford a practical demonstration, corroborating, in the most convincing manner, the truth at which we have arrived.

It would be easy to multiply proofs until the mind would lose in their number the perception of their weight, but we forbear. To the unbiased reason a voice from heaven, proclaiming in the tones of the arch-angel himself the utter, inveterate, and eternal hatred of Christ toward those things, could not add to the weight of evidence already afforded, and if any person is not convinced, it is because the perverse nature *will* not be.

These indulgences are in complete hostility to the nature of Christ. They violate the whole scope and tenor of the sacred scriptures; the statements of which, in analogous cases, are invariably condemnatory; their effect upon christian character is evil and only evil, and that continually; the Holy Spirit denounces and prohibits them; and finally, the word of God as clearly and as explicitly as language can speak, utters its prohibitions. If these all fail to express His mind, *the very stones must cry out!*

CHAPTER II.

THE second question propounded in the present essay is, What is the effect of such adorning upon the Individual, the Church, and the World?

Ans. I. The effect upon the Individual.

First. It squanders the means which God has given for better purposes, and for which he will hold every one to the strictest accountability.

"The earth is the Lord's, and the fullness thereof." "The silver and the gold are his." We poor mortals have nothing, *absolutely nothing*, in our own right. We are stewards of the Lord's treasures, and that which we possess is only loaned us for a time, that we may "make to ourselves friends of the mammon of unrighteousness, that we may be received at last into everlasting habitations."

Statistics show that for every eighteen dollars expended in the M. E. Church in her benevolent enterprises, and the support of the ministry, one soul is converted. If any thing near the same ratio exists in other churches, with what accusing voices do our empty missionary treasuries plead, as their mighty claims, freighted with immortal destinies, are turned aside by the gift of the silver dime, when tens or hundreds of golden dollars might be substituted by casting the useless and forbidden adornments at the foot of the cross.

Many christian women bear constantly upon their persons useless ornaments enough to sustain a missionary and his family in the most distant portions of the work. To such the example of the ancient Israelites is worthy of all imitation. "And Aaron said unto them, Break off the golden earrings which *are* in the ears of your wives, of your sons, and of your daughters, and bring *them* unto me." (Exodus, xxxii: 2.) "And they came, both men and women, as many as were willing hearted, *and* brought bracelets, and earrings, and rings, and tablets, all jewels of gold; and every man that offered, *offered* an offering of gold unto the Lord." (Ex. xxxv: 22.) "We have therefore brought an oblation for the Lord, what every man hath gotten, of jewels of gold, chains, and bracelets, rings, earrings, and tablets, to make an atonement for our souls before the Lord." (Num. xxxi: 50.)

For ourself, we can but question the piety or the education of that person who habitually expends double or treble the amount really needed for personal adornments and dress, while objects of charity throng on every side.

God has not so arranged the affairs of life, that our expenditures must seek the distributing energies of extravagance in default of the opportunities implied in Prov. xi: 25. "The liberal soul shall be made fat: and he that watereth shall be watered also himself;" or in Isa., lviii: 10. "And *if* thou draw out thy soul to the hungry, and satisfy the afflicted soul, then shall thy light rise in obscurity, and thy darkness *be* as the noonday." No, no. The lap of want is spread beside the pathway of the most favored daughter of luxury, and she need not even step aside to cast her offerings upon it. From every one who has a heart to feel for human wo, and a hand able to give a "silver lining" to the dark clouds of sorrowing destitution, God has a right to expect a hearty response to his suggestive injunction, "Withhold not good from them to whom it is due, when it is in the power of thine hand to do *it.*

Say not unto thy neighbor, Go, and come again, and to-morrow I will give, when thou hast it by thee." (Prov., iii: 27, 28.) He does require it, and the recording angel writes against every dollar expended for mere ornament, or to procure costlier apparel than is actually needed, the bitter condemnation, It was *squandered.*

Squandered, though pity wept; squandered, though benevolence remonstrated; squandered, though religion frowned; squandered, though responsibility trembled; squandered, though sympathy chilled within; *squandered* because Pride and Fashion bade. O, cursed Pride!—O, Fashion! gay enchanters, wiling to the pit—ye handmaids of perdition! God save his children from your snares!

Another effect upon the individual of such adornment, is, that—

It misspends his time. "A minister, calling to visit a lady, was detained a long time while she was dressing. At length she made her appearance, bedizened in all the frippery of fashion and folly. The minister was in tears. She asked the cause of his grief; when he replied, 'I weep, madam, to think, that an immortal being should spend so much of that precious time which was given her to prepare for eternity, in thus vainly adorning that body which must so soon become a prey to worms.'"

The reproof in this instance was blessed to the conversion of the lady. But, alas! how many pass on to the dying hour, without the rebuke, and destitute of its benefits. One such exclaimed to several ministers who came to comfort her, "Call back time again. If you can call back time again, then there may be hope for me. But time is gone." How bitter must be the reflections which the strange excitements of the departing hour force upon the spirit that has allowed time to run away in the gay pursuits of fashion, or in decking the perishing body with the emblazoned heraldries of the kingdom of darkness. How scathing such a retrospect of life. Time's sands run out and time's work all undone! How appalling the visions that gather in dim and shadowy outline just beyond the portals of the grave!

When we remember that time is given to us for the noblest of purposes, and that, at the best, it is fearfully curtailed by a thousand nameless circumstances that occupy the mind for the passing instant, it becomes a question of serious moment, how best to improve what remains to us. We may scarcely be said to begin to live the real responsible life of the world until the age of fifteen. Supposing then that we survive the average length of human life, we have but fifteen more in which to work out the mighty problem of future destiny.

But when we subtract from this the time consumed in sleeping, eating, domestic duties, and the necessary socialities of life, we are narrowed down to three or four hours a day for the most favored, and scarcely a single one for those not so well situated, as the utmost that can be devoted to the concerns of the soul. Now, if from that single hour three-fourths be separated for a painfully precise and finical toilet, which might just as well have been accomplished in other hours, how fearfully does it abridge the Bible lesson, the private prayer, and the self-examination necessary to a holy life. And is there no wrong in this? Behold ye have robbed God: this whole people have robbed God. "But ye say, Wherein have we robbed thee? In tithes and offerings." Ah, should the ghosts of all these murdered hours rise before the astonished gaze of that careless fair one, as she prinks and trims beside their new made graves in her own dressing room, how soon would she cast aside the suicidal employment. It is no wonder that personal piety dwindles to such puerile results. It is no wonder that a powerless, cold, dead formalism possesses the church. In labored attempts to win compliments from some dandy fool, or from some circle of silly and stupid self-spoiled worldlings, time enough is spent every year by thousands who name the name of Christ, to pray a dozen souls to heaven. Yes, if it were possible, to take them there even in Elijah's chariot of fire. How many are now mourning over their coldness and want of joy, who, if they would spend but one-fourth of the time each day in private religious devotion that they now do in private and most intense devotion to the goddess of Fashion, would soon shine as lights in the world, instead of emitting the feeble and sickly glare which only lures others to destruction and misery. Thousands upon thousands in our land are daily in this very way enlisting, body and soul, in the army of evil, and by their influence seeking recruits for satan's service and doom among the gay around them. Would to God they were less successful.

The very thought that the godlike powers of the immortal soul are prostituted to purposes so far beneath its dignity, and that too in the bright morning of life, when it should be ranging aloft, dwelling upon the grandeur of its eternal destiny, and gathering its energies for the mighty sweep of time toward the judgment, the thought that *then* its precious moments should be thus occupied, and its lofty nature cramped and fettered, and hoodwinked, and paralyzed, O, it is too much to realize in all its terrible extent of degradation!

Simply as a method of employing the activities of the soul, aside from all consideration of its results, it should meet the most severe reprehension from every lover of his fellow. The silly peacock may expand his tail and strut about in contemplation of its beauties, and it does just what we may expect. For the adornment is one which God has given, and the employment is on a level with the powers bestowed. But for "godlike" man and "angelic" woman to adopt the customs of barbarians, and imagine that they are dignified by gold, and gems, and costly attire, and that the arrangement of these is the hight of their mental and spiritual aspirations, exhibits far too low an estimate of human worth.

An other consequence of this practice is, that—

It perverts the judgment.

There can be no right judgment except there be exemption from the bias of prejudice. But prejudice is a necessary consequence of a corrupted will and a selfish nature, both of which are, more or less, involved in the habit of adornment. The well-known lines—

> "A man, convinced against his will,
> Is of the same opinion still,"

express a truth in the phenomena of mind, against which we can not close our eyes, and form a fitting preface to the declaration of Holy Writ, "There is a way that seemeth right unto a man, but the end thereof *are* the ways of death." A person may be sincere in a wrong belief, at the time of avowing it, but there has previously been the basest treachery to his moral nature, to produce the blindness. Innocence in the possession of a belief, and sincerity in that belief, are not necessarily conjoined. Pride, and selfishness, and corrupt will, may have educated the judgment into the way which it now approves, but from which it may once have shrunk in deepest abhorrence. Nor is this so laborious a work as might be supposed. The path of moral deterioration is a down-hill road, and may have little to prevent the smoothness of its progress.

The soil, which has been carefully cultivated and weeded, needs only a little neglect to cause a perverted growth of thistles to spring up. So it is with man. Perversion is a growth of man's fallen nature, and needs the exterminating hand of holy purposes and divine affections to supplant it, while selfishness would only foster its development. Perhaps some who read this essay will not be convinced, after all the evidence that has been adduced, that habits of adornment are wrong. If so, we point to their own position as proof of what we have just affirmed.

An other result of this habit, subordinate to the foregoing, is this: It establishes a false standard of Taste.

The perversion, in this case, consists in an

erroneous judgment of the beautiful. All true beauty is the result of a nice adaptation of the means used to produce it, to the nature and circumstances of the object to be adorned. When angels are depicted, they always appear in modest female loveliness, or in the noble beauty of manhood in its purity, but are never adorned with the glittering tinsel of fashion's drapery.

The intuitive perception of our reason, in reference to them, at least, supports the sentiment—

> "Beauty, when unadorned, adorned the most."

For we feel that that which constitutes their beauty inheres within, belongs to their essential spirituality. How strangely do we forget that the same rule applies to ourselves. And the perversion lies, not in over-estimating the inherent value of beauty, or the good which it confers, but in transferring it from the essential spirituality to a mere accident of its existence, or, in other words, from mind to matter.

We would not teach the young to despise either beauty or its adventitious aids, but we would have them learn that its highest forms in man, as in angels, consist in the adornments of the mind and the spirit. Whenever, then, the outward form is made to assume the rights and privileges of mind, in this respect, it is a perversion of judgment, lamentable nct only in itself, but because of its evil influence upon every other interest connected with this subject. To illustrate. The mind, thus perverted, can not readily be made to feel the sinfulness of such indulgence, because it has fortified itself behind a supposed necessity for adornment, assuming that the body, and not the mind, is the fit subject of its efforts. For the same reason, the claims of benevolence can not be honored. Thus we might pass over all the moral virtues, and show that the warping power of this perverted judgment, by erecting a false standard of truth, falls with crushing influence upon each.

But the standard which is recognized is not merely false, it is also degrading. The statuary which arrests and enchains a world's admiration, is never adorned in the glittering gewgaws of worldly pride. But the figures in those paintings which are hung up in certain places on purpose to degrade and inflame the imagination, and excite the passions of the unwary, as well as their living originals as they walk forth to lure their victims to "the way that takes hold on hell;" these are, as is well known, invested with the adornments needful for their work. A word to the wise is sufficient.

Again, this habit cultivates selfishness, and corrupts the will.

The principle of selfishness is, perhaps, the strongest exhibition of depravity that human nature furnishes. While it has in itself no element of good, and is powerless to bestow blessings upon its possessor, it is the fruitful seed of many vices fatal to the happiness of the individual, to the peace of society, and to the progress of the cause of Christ. In its essence and in all its forms, it is opposed to that true love and that genuine benevolence which the religion of Christ imparts, and in the possession of which alone can man be prepared to dwell with God, who himself is Love.

Hence the renunciation of selfishness is enjoined, as a first principle, in christian experience. The passage which has been already quoted, "Ye are not your own, for ye are bought with a price; therefore, glorify God in your body and in your spirit, which are God's," is an authoritative statement of the truth; and the inference from the declaration "therefore glorify God," etc., is a mandatory summary of our obligations. The common reason of mankind has united with the Bible in the condemnation of the evil, and, though it has had no power sufficient to restrain its workings, still recognizes the desirableness of such restraint in the whole code of social politeness and formal etiquette.

In theory, society scorns the epithet of selfishness, and leaves boors and savages to wallow in its degrading associations. Were it unrepressed, earth would soon become a pandemonium more dreadful than ever poet's vision saw, or artist's colors painted. Yet so spontaneous and active is it in the human breast, that, notwithstanding the condemnation of reason and religion, and the superadded experience of its bitterness, it still lives in countless forms of disgusting loathsomeness. It must be evident, then, to every one, that any thing having a tendency to cultivate a principle so destructive, must be wrong, and should be carefully avoided.

We have asserted that indulgences in display have such a tendency, and it can be easily shown that such is the energy of their influence as to rise even to the position of a *direct educational power.* The appeal may first be made to surface facts, patent to the observation of every one. We see persons in every walk of life using the means which are actually needed for the good of others dependent upon them, in procuring the adornments of pride. Parents limit the education of their children, because their expenditures for dress and ornament are so great that it can not be afforded. Church members curtail their subscription for the support of the ministry, and leave their pastors to toil on in straightened circumstances and with care-burdened minds, because of their own useless indulgences. Rings, bracelets, pins, and costly robes, etc., are purchased instead of the useful book. The expenditure of two dollars extra on a new garment excludes the religious newspaper. The payment of one hundred dollars for watch and chain reduces the subscription to some benevolent society fifty dollars for the year. Thus runs the evil. What is it but selfishness in all its naked deformity, if stripped of the fancied *necessity* which Fashion throws around it? Necessity indeed! The silly dupes may blind themselves and others who are akin of spirit, but the degrading subterfuge is too transparent to satisfy for a single instant the demands of humanity, much less the claims of perjured honesty and outraged piety. Away with the hypocritical cant, and at least have the manhood to declare your preference for selfish indulgences over the pleasurable duties of benevolence, over the gospel obligations relative to the ministry, over all the self-denying efforts of religion.

Corruption of the will must also be a result. There is indeed no doubt that this faculty has much to do in forming the habit. But the indulgence of the habit has a reflex influence in corrupting still farther the voluntary power, till a *habit* of sinful determination relative to this subject is formed.

Such is the complex nature of the mind, and such the mutual influence of its faculties, that selfishness can never be indulged except at the expense of a burdened conscience and a corrupted will. Hence it is that men become more and more hardened by long persistence in evil practices, until it seems in some cases an open question whether conscience is not totally paralyzed, and the will so depraved that it has lost all power of choosing the right.

In the same manner, though not to the same extent, the experience of those who have conscientious scruples about adornment, in their hours of deeper religious feeling, and who lose them with declining piety, illustrates the great fact that every forbidden indulgence corrupts the will. When the will is yielding under the presence of religious emotions, the mind is awake to the responsibility of the habit, but no sooner does its native corruption resume a portion of its sway, than returning insensibility evidences its fearful progress in the downward way. It may be held as an axiom in mental philosophy, that every development of selfishness corrupts the will, and prepares it for some greater exhibition of its depravity. Then when that development is the consequence not merely of an *act* but of an established *habit*, its deteriorating influence is in the ratio of its own strength and permanence. If, in other respects, the practice of adornment is inexpedient and hazardous, in this it is absolutely suicidal. It is a voluntary degradation of the voluntary power, a willful choosing of the wrong, with the full consciousness that the choice perpetuates itself by rendering it more and more difficult even to prefer the right.

Selfishness being thus cultured and the will thus corrupted, the way is prepared for another evil. That is,

The excitement of the passions.

The love of display may become so absorbing that its *own* most proper designation is *passion*. And that passion in many cases rushes to the fearful verge of moral madness. How many, when once they have entered upon the career of fashionable dissipation, have found no halting place, even though religion, and affection, and reason, and self-preservation, cried in their ears, until bankruptcy, and ruined health, and a dissolute family have brought them to their senses just in time to see the wreck which their insane extravagance had spread around them, and then to sink to an unwelcome grave, or else, as frail and shattered vanities to live on, the mere foam of existence, cursed and cursing till they die.

This result is no doubt largely attributable to the fact before stated, viz: the false judgment of the beautiful. Beauty, unless intrinsic, depends, to a great extent, upon the laws of association. So long as an article of apparel is confined to the circle of the noble, wealthy, and refined, it is considered tasteful, but no sooner does it begin its downward course through the various ranks of society, than it presents itself in every conceivable association, and is at once placed under the ban of a cultivated taste. Hence arises the necessity of the frequent changes in Fashion. These changes, recurring so often, engross so much of the time and attention, that at length the habit of solicitude respecting them becomes paramount to every other, and the poor deluded victim presents the sad spectacle of a half demented "butterfly of Fashion."

"During the occupancy of the city of Moscow by the French army, a party of officers and soldiers determined to have a military levee, and for this purpose chose the deserted palace of a nobleman, in the vault of which a large quantity of powder had been deposited. That night the city was set on fire. As the sun went down they began to assemble. The females who followed the fortunes of the French forces were decorated for the occasion. The gayest and noblest of the army were there, and merriment reigned over the crowd. During the dance the fire rapidly approached them; they saw it coming, but felt no fear. At length the building next to the one which they occupied was on fire. Coming to the windows, they gazed upon the billows of fire which swept upon their fortress, and then returned to their amusement. Again and again they left their amusement to watch the progress of the flames. At length the dance ceased, and the necessity of leaving the scene of merriment became apparent to all. They were enveloped in a flood of fire, and gazed on with deep and awful solemnity. At length the fire, communicating to their own building, caused them to prepare for flight, when a brave young officer named Carnot, waved his jeweled glove above his head, and exclaimed, 'One dance more, and defiance to the flames.' All caught the enthusiasm of the moment, and 'one dance more and defiance to the flames,' burst from the lips of all. The dance commenced. Louder and louder grew the sound of music, and faster and faster fell the pattering footsteps of dancing men and women, when suddenly they heard a cry, 'The fire has reached the magazine! Fly! Fly for life!' One moment they stood transfixed with horror—they did not know the magazine was there—and ere they recovered from their stupor, the vault exploded, the building was shattered to pieces, and the dancers were hurried into a fearful eternity."

How fitly does this represent the fearful commercial conflagration that is now sweeping with such desolating fury over the world. Men were warned of its approach. They gazed upon the nearing flames. But they turned again to their pleasures, till involved in the general crash of ruin. More than one firm of heavy capital and abundant resources, has failed, for want of a few hundred dollars, which but a short time previously had been wasted in some fashionable extravagance. But such was the intoxicating power of the indulgence, that the bewildered victims whirled on like the giddy dancers, till the retributions of a righteous providence arrested their career.

Not only does it develop the passion of display, but with it envy, jealousy, pride, evil speaking, hypocrisy, covetousness, hatred, and discontent. When once the passion for adornment takes possession of the mind, the more fortunate devotee is envied with an intensity proportioned to her success. Jealousy watches with an evil eye and a slanderous tongue every movement of a rival. Hypocrisy waits with cringing flattery and self-degrading duplicity, in the halls of the pampered millionaire. Covetousness gloats upon his gathered stores. Hatred watches the gains of others in hope that fire or flood will destroy them. And all combined fan high the flames of discontent. Such is the retinue of sinful adornment. If they do not all appear in every case, praise not the habit for the exemption. Would you laud the cup because all who quaff its sparkling cheer do not die drunkards? Neither does the fact that other causes have repressed a portion of the evil, give ground for the judgment of charity. "But if ye have bitter envying and strife in your hearts, glory not, and lie not against the truth. This wisdom descendeth not from above, but *is* earthly, sensual, devilish. For where envying and strife *is*, there *is* confusion and every evil work. But the wisdom that is from above is first pure, then peaceable, gentle, *and* easy to be entreated, full of mercy and good fruits, without partiality, and without hypocrisy." (James, iii. 14–17.)

Bad as is the representation made above, it does not reach the whole truth. There are facts which may not be told in the ears of all. There is a way that takes hold on hell. And when vice allures the strongest, it is when arrayed in the trappings of luxurious vanity. When virtue is most tempted, it is when beguiled by charms whose setting is the blinding witchery of Fashion's drapery and the glittering enticements of gem-decked pleasures.

Again, this habit chills the sympathies, hardens the heart, and degrades the mind.

It is a law of mind, that the exhibition of mock sympathy, or the exercise of real sympathy to an excessive degree in known cases of no real importance, is chilling and ultimately destructive to sympathy itself. Hence it is that novel-reading, by its excitement of the sympathies when it is known that there is no reality answering to the sympathetic emotion, is so injurious to the mental and moral nature. So with the practice under review. It is notorious that a rent collar, or spotted dress, or broken article of jewelry, will call forth condolence enough to bury one in sympathy, when the possessor is quite probably thanking her stars for the accident, because it will afford a good excuse to get an other. A beggar at the door will be turned away that very hour, with many self righteous and pert remarks about the "impropriety of encouraging street beggars," etc.

As justly, as keenly has "Nothing to wear" satirized a similar disposition.

"Still an other, whose tortures have been most terrific,
Even since the sad loss of the steamer *Pacific*,
In which were ingulfed, not friend or relation,
(For whose fate she perhaps might have found consolation,
Or borne it, at least, with serene resignation,)
But the choicest assortment of French sleeves and collars,
Ever sent out from Paris, worth thousands of dollars,
And all as to style most *recherché* and rare,
The want of which leaves her with nothing to wear,
And renders her life so drear and dyspeptic
That she's quite a recluse, and almost a skeptic,
For she touchingly says that this sort of grief
Can not find in Religion the slightest relief,
And philosophy has not a maxim to spare
For the victims of such overwhelming despair."

Again, when speaking

" Of those fossil remains which she called her 'affections,'
And that rather decayed, but well-known work of art,
Which Miss Flora persisted in styling 'her heart,"

he has well painted the results of such indulgence.

And in proportion to the deadening of the natural sympathies, is that insensibility to the influences of the Holy Spirit, which is hardness of the heart and reprobacy of mind. In a world of suffering like ours, we can but deplore any thing that tends to repress the spontaneous outgushings of the fraternal feeling which the benevolent Creator has placed in each human bosom. We can but regard every such attempt as an attack upon the vital interests of society that should never be tolerated. "Rejoice with them that do rejoice, and weep with them that weep." (Rom. xii: 15.) "Put on therefore, as the elect of God, holy and beloved, bowels of mercies, kindness, humbleness of mind, meeknesss, long-suffering, forbearing one another, and forgiving one another, if any man have a quarrel against any: even as Christ forgave you, so also *do* ye. And above all these things *put on* charity, which is the bond of perfectness. And let the peace of God rule in your hearts, to the which also ye are called in one body; and be ye thankful. Let the word of Christ dwell in you richly in all wisdom; teaching and admonishing one another in psalms and hymns and spiritual songs, singing with grace in your hearts to the Lord. And whatsoever ye do in word or deed, *do* all in the name of the Lord Jesus, giving thanks to God and the Father by him." (Col. iii: 12-17.) These passages contain the Bible rule and measure of the grace, with its associate manifestations. Compare these statements with the frivolity, selfishness, and recklessness, connected with a confirmed habit of adornment, and you have in their essential antagonism a proof of the chilling influence which it must exert upon true sympathy. And when added to all this is a growing insensibility to the only influence that can stem the tide of ruin and regenerate the nature, we have one of the most complete pictures of the desperate depravity of the heart and the reckless daring of consequences, that the sad history of humanity affords within the ranks of respectable society. It is no wonder that poets and romance writers have stigmatized "the world," i. e., the fashionable world, as "heartless." In doing so, they have recorded not merely the impression which the outward appearance would give, but they have analyzed the inner sources of thought and feeling, and characterized them in accordance with the effect that naturally ensues to themselves from this course of life. Heartless they are, not merely in reference to the great interests of humanity, but as regards the mighty claims which crowd upon us in connection with the scheme of redemption by our Lord Jesus Christ.

As a necessary corollary from all that precedes, it must follow that—

The habit of display degrades the mind.

Nor is it a degradation merely in theory, or in the eyes of those who note all tendencies with philosophic precision, and weigh them with scientific care. It is a *self-conscious* humiliation, all the more galling as it is felt to be folly. The worldling may for a time remain unconscious of the mighty powers within him, and may forget his destiny, but vanities and dreams will not always satisfy the earnest longings of the immortal nature, and sometimes he will awaken to the fact that he is passing through this land of shadows to one of realities too substantial to be evaded, and then he knows, he *feels* for the moment, how degrading to all the nobler instincts of his being, is such a life of "painted outsides and hollow pretenses." But alas! as "the dog *is* turned to his own vomit again; and the sow that was washed, to her wallowing in the mire," so turns his soul again to pleasure's circles, that her deeper draught may drown his fears, and stupify his consciousness of a hereafter. Thus a deeper degradation follows close upon the recollection of the one that has gone before, until he becomes in reality fit for little else than to be preserved for a time as are the abnormal members of the human frame, to be a warning to others.

But the guilt of such voluntary disarrangement of the handiwork of the Almighty, such willful enslavement of all the immortal powers of the blood-bought soul, who shall estimate? Since the moral suicide is as complete, we see no difference between "life drained drop by drop from the soul, and that sent forth at a blow from the red hand." Many have died upon the gallows for crime committed in the heat of momentary passion, with far less real degradation of the moral nature, and less willful criminality before God, than must be attached to the character of one who deliberately SQUANDERS MEANS, MISSPENDS TIME, PERVERTS THE JUDGMENT, CULTIVATES SELFISHNESS, CORRUPTS THE WILL, EXCITES THE PASSIONS, CHILLS THE SYMPATHIES, HARDENS THE HEART, DEGRADES THE MIND, AND ALL FOR SO POOR A MOTIVE AND FOR SO TRANSIENT AND DECEPTIVE A REWARD.

The habit of paying undue attention to trifles when things of real importance demand the thought, is always deteriorating to the mental constitution, and if long persisted in, unfits it to take calm and proper views of the real interests of existence, or to struggle successfully with the evils of the world. Few greater misfortunes can befall a youth than to be trained into the belief that dress and appearance are the supreme good after which to aspire, and the chief responsibilities of probation. To allow silks and satins, sleeves and collars, shawls and ermine, lace and jewelry, etc., to engross the attention, when all the powers of the soul should be engaged in the grand struggle for an imperishable crown, is necessarily disarranging to the order of mental action, destructive to the proper balance of the powers (*which even safety from crime demands*), and effectually nullifying to the claims of God. Can it be expected, then, that God shall be unmindful of this thing?

We have intimated that safety from crime demands the proper balance of the mental powers. This truth will need very little elucidation. If the passions usurp the authority of the conscience, and the mandates of Fashion are esteemed of higher authority than the will of God, it is plain that the law of progression which controls all our activities, must point toward an alliance with evil at some future stage of the descending road, which will be marked by a development of the passions audacious in a degree commensurate with their increased strength. What the crime then developed shall be, may depend much upon circumstances, but the tendency to *some* crime lies within the very nature of self-degradation. Even if the tendency never grows into an actual commission of criminal acts, it will be because of counteracting influences.

When to this we add the weight of considerations still to be urged, it must be plain to every mind that a gradual steeling of the mind against all good influences is an attendant phenomenon of the retrogression, and that the soul is thus left defenseless and powerless amid the tendencies to ruin surrounding it. Now place such a mind amid the dissipations and follies, and hypocrisies of fashionable life; let the social affections and sympathies be scathed, and the conscience silenced, and the passions excited; let it be the demoralizing fact that *wealth* instead of *character* is the standard of respectability; let the rake and the debauchee be the admitted companions and equals; let all this be so, and then must human nature be something more than it is, if virtue's strongest temptations lie not concealed amid the opportunities which waltzes at late hours, and their kindred amusements, so sedulously present.

Again, this habit causes the violation of the most solemn religious vows.

Such vows have been made at times unnumbered in the history of every professing christian. In the bitterness of penitential emotion, while drinking the "wormwood and the gall," they were lisped forth in the chamber of secret prayer, or in utter wretchedness groaned out upon the midnight couch of torturing reflections.

"I'll go to Jesus, though my sin
Like mountains round me close;
I know his courts, I'll enter in,
Whatever may oppose.

"Prostrate I'll lie before his throne,
And there my guilt confess;
I'll tell him I'm a wretch undone
Without his sov'reign grace.

"I can but perish if I go,
I am resolved to try;
For, if I stay away, I know
I must for ever die."

Then followed the act of solemn consecration.

"Nay, but I yield, I yield;
I can hold out no more;
I sink, by dying love compelled,
And own thee conqueror.

"Though late, I all forsake;
My friends, my all resign;
Gracious Redeemer, take, O take,
And seal me ever thine."

Then when the mighty work was done, how joyfully they sang—

"He justly claims us for his own,
Who bought us with a price;
The christian lives to Christ alone,
To Christ alone he dies.

"Jesus, thine own at last receive;
Fulfill our heart's desire;
And let us to thy glory live,
And in thy cause expire.

"Our souls and bodies we resign;
With joy we render thee
Our all—no longer ours, but thine,
To all eternity."

And repeatedly, as gratitude has swelled their bosoms, have they exclaimed—

"If so poor a worm as I
May to thy great glory live,
All my actions sanctify,
All my words and thoughts receive;
Claim me for thy service, claim
All I have and all I am.

"Take my soul and body's powers;
Take my mem'ry, mind, and will;
All my goods and all my hours;
All I know, and all I feel;
All I think, or speak, or do;
Take my heart, but make it new."

When receiving the symbols of the broken body and shed blood of our Lord, their language has been—

"Thou God of covenanted grace,
Hear and record my vow,
While in thy courts I seek thy face,
And at thine altar bow.

"Henceforth to thee myself I give,
With single heart and eye,
To walk before thee while I live,
And bless thee when I die."

And ofttimes when coldness has long held them, but they have at length aroused from their lethargy, they have joined in the expressions—

"Thine would I live, thine would I die;
Be thine through all eternity;
The vow is passed beyond repeal,
And now I set the solemn seal.

"Here at that cross where flows the blood
That bought my guilty soul for God,
Thee my new Master now I call,
And consecrate to thee my all."

And as returning joys have brightened their hopes of heaven, O, with what heartiness have they cried—

"'T is done, the great transaction's done;
I am my Lord's and he is mine;
He drew me, and I followed on,
Charmed to confess the voice divine.

"Now rest, my long divided heart;
Fixed on this blissful center, rest;
Nor ever from thy Lord depart;
With him of every good possessed."

"High Heaven, that heard the solemn vow,
That vow renewed shall daily hear,
Till in life's latest hour I bow,
And bless in death a bond so dear."

In that deeply interesting moment when, in the baptismal rite, they took upon themselves the solemn obligation to live as his covenant people, they promised to "renounce the devil and all his works, the vain pomp and glory of the world, with all covetous desires of the same, and the carnal desires of the flesh, so as not to follow or be led by them." "A condition of church membership is that the candidate shall have been baptized, and, of course, by plain implication, is living in the performance of the baptismal vow. This vow can never be innocently broken with God, because founded upon unchanging rights. And it is a compact with the church universal in baptism, and with the particular branch of the church with which the candidate united, which can never be repealed."

Thus does the practice of adornment not only violate all the consecration vows of penitence and of gratitude—vows which have been made in the most trying circumstances of life; that have been repeated when bending over the suffering form of some loved one, or when wiping the death-damps from the brow of some cherished hope, or when gazing into the cold and cheerless grave of some blighted affection—not only all these does it disregard, but it holds the solemn compacts of church relationship as things of naught.

True, those who are thus guilty may endeavor to extenuate their fault. "Perhaps there is no sophism more generally acted upon than this. 'The obligations of an individual are measured by his character.' For example, the backslider considers himself exempt from christian duty, because he does not possess the christian character. It is a great mistake. Obligations are eternal and immutable, and no change of character can ever abrogate them. We thence conclude, that such vows and compacts can never be innocently broken. Yet every person who practices what we condemn in this article, is guilty of the violation of his baptismal vow, and his vow of church relationship. Let such tell us upon what principle they claim the honor of the christian name, while they still persist in such a course." (Gift of Power, p. 262.)

"Offer unto God thanksgiving; and pay thy vows unto the Most High." (Ps. 50, 14.) "When thou vowest a vow unto God, defer not to pay it; for *he hath* no pleasure in fools: pay that which thou hast vowed. Better *is it* that thou shouldst not vow, than that thou shouldst vow and not pay. Suffer not thy mouth to cause thy flesh to sin; neither say thou before the angel, that it *was* an error: wherefore should God be angry at thy voice, and destroy the work of thine hands?" (Eccl. v: 4–6.)

Another consequence of the practice of adornment is that—

It creates a habit of sinful indulgence.

It has been well said, "We paint our lives in fresco. The soft and facile plaster of the moment hardens under every stroke of the brush into eternal rock." Truthfully and beautifully does this express the power of habit. Every word and every thought is shaping the soul into some form of activity or repose, which, if strengthened to a given point, will remain as unchangeable as the decrees of fate.

The muscles of the human frame may be trained by the influence of habit to an almost incredible degree of vigor and endurance. A Turkish porter will trot at a rapid pace, and carry a weight of six hundred pounds. "Milo, a celebrated athlete of Crotona, in Italy, accustomed himself to carry the greatest burdens, and by degrees became a monster in strength. It is said that he carried on his shoulder an ox four years old, weighing upward of one thousand pounds, and afterward killed him with one blow of his fist. He was seven times crowned at the Pythian games, and six at the Olympic. He presented himself the seventh time, but no one had the courage to enter the list against him. He was one of the disciples of Pythagoras, and to his uncommon strength that learned preceptor and his pupils owed their lives. The pillar that supported the roof of the building suddenly gave way, but Milo supported the roof of the house, and gave the philosopher time to escape."

So with the mind. By slow and imperceptible degrees it may be molded to any course of action, and confirmed in the effort until its activities shall run to it as readily as they did originally in their natural channels, and with even greater strength.

Habit is stronger than nature. It becomes then a question of serious moment. What *habits* are our actions forming? The voice of desire listened to once, prepares the ear for a second audience. The prohibited pleasure gazed upon to-day, leaves a little of its attraction for the display of to-morrow. The sinful indulgence which now courts favor once smiled upon, it will grow with rolling years, till the humble beggar of your clemency shall lord it over reason, conscience, *all*, and till you shall find yourself the bond slave of a tyranny as degrading as at the outset it was insignificant.

> "Vice is a monster of so frightful mien,
> As, to be hated, needs but to be seen;
> Yet seen too oft, familiar with her face,
> We first endure, then pity, then embrace."

This is the philosophy of the habit of indulgence created by the practice of adornment. When first entered upon it is with faltering accents and trembling steps. But soon the step is firmer and the tones more full. At last with reckless haste and wild impassioned notes, the course is rushed over till it ends in ruin and death.

One such habit of indulgence formed, and the rash experimenter is moving down the slope where every gratification adds momentum to his progress, and each acceleration of velocity brings with it the luring power of some other sin lying right along his pathway. These combined excite the appetite for some still untasted sweet of pleasure, till habit is interwoven with habit, sin interfused with sin, and all interpenetrated with corruption. Then how hard, O how hard for him to check his career, and retrace his steps up the long, toilsome steep of self-denying effort and cross-bearing activity.

Let me here address the young and gay. You expect to prepare for death at some future time, and are fully conscious that your present conduct is not leading you toward that preparation. On the contrary, if you have serious impressions you are well aware that a few follies will effectually dissipate them. Now let me ask, Where is the foundation of your hope of turning one day to God? If now, in the spring time of life, with your hearts free from the cares of the world, untrammelled by the sinful habits of long years, unburdened with the guilt of age, if now, with all these favorable circumstances, you deliberately slight the instructions of your sabbath school, and if, in spite of the remonstrances of your conscience, and the strivings of the Spirit, you calmly, deliberately, and with purpose forsworn, cast yourself into the eddying tide of fashionable indulgences, mar your character by the cultivation of selfishness, by the corruption of your will, by the perversion of your judgment, by the excitement of your passions, and, by the creation of habits of sinful indulgence, and, in addition, load yourself with the guilt of squandered means, and misspent time, and broken vows; if you willfully do all this, where is the foundation of your hope that while the whirl of the life-dance is about you, you will turn from the evil of your ways and seek after God? And even if by some rare providence, with all these fearful odds against you, you should be brought to reflection, is it wise, is it prudent, is it *safe*, to lay up such a magazine of material for the life-struggle that is to follow? O, the bitter groans that the breaking of those habits will then cost;

the intense, fearful, desperate struggle with your own nature that then must be; the vain regrets, the grief-wrung prayers, the legion of discouragements, and all this when but a few short steps from the darkness of the GRAVE. O, beware, beware! The voice of the siren may be sweet, and the form of the enchantress may be decked in nameless beauties, but remember that her silver tones speak naught but lies, her gorgeous drapery is but the semblance of a dream. Her bowers may be fragrant with the richest perfume, they may be fanned by the softest zephyrs, they may be jubilant with soul-stirring strains. But the perfumes will prove to be but the odor which poisons as it pleases, the breezes will bear miasma on their breath, the jubilant strains will be the sounds of joy never to be realized.

The first habit of sinful indulgence is the temporal and eternal ruin of all those whose transgressions are visited upon them here. The culprit upon the gallows, the criminal in the prison, and the wretch whom justice still allows to run at large, were made what they have become by the first habit of sinful indulgence. A fearful thing it is to tamper with the moral virtues of the soul. Like vestal fires they should be guarded with pious zeal, and the hand that should dare to smother one of them should meet the bitter execration which its sacrilege would deserve.

As a consequence of the foregoing, the habit of adornment—

Increases the love of the world.

This proposition may be denied, but a moment's reflection will be sufficient to convince the objector, that if one sympathizes to such an extent with the world as to choose its livery and desire its associations, these things, by the inevitable laws of mind, will deepen that sympathy into love. There is something so weakening to the christian graces in the fact of being placed under false colors, that the inconsistency of *being* in such a position is forgotten in the dread of the further inconsistency of *being exhibited* in the midst of such associations. Hence these graces are trimmed down to the low standard of worldly formalism, while the love of the world triumphs in their defeat, and rises by their fall.

A poor thing to love is this world, and small is the merit of any attempt to make us love it better, especially since it is in open competition with the love of Christ.

Every action has a tendency to make us love the world more, or Christ better, and no action can increase our love for both. Now, if the practice of adornment does deepen our piety and quicken our zeal, we have nothing more to say. If it does not do this, it must tend to the opposite, as experience and scripture declare that it always does. "Know ye not that the friendship of the world is at enmity with God? Whosoever therefore will be a friend of the world is the enemy of God." (James, iv: 4.)

Again, the habit of adornment enslaves the conscience.

This it does by impeaching the authority of heaven in what it pleases to term unimportant matters, and by rendering life a continuous chain of habitual transgressions. There is no more common error than the supposition that the enormity of our offenses is gauged by our estimate of them. With God there is no comparative scale of transgression, except as our sins concern the interests of our fellow-men. We may contract as much guilt by a so-called little sin as by many which rank higher among men upon the category of crime. The authority of a lawgiver may be as much questioned by a minor transgression as by one that involves more extended interests. Hence the declaration, "Whosoever shall keep the whole law, and yet offend in one *point*, he is guilty of all." (James, ii: 10.)

When the Rubicon is once passed, though but a step beyond may have been taken, the soul is committed to evil as certainly as though it were left far in the rear, yet then the flattering unction is laid to that soul that all is right. Because the stream has proved so narrow, it would fain believe that it has not been crossed at all, while in fact it stands upon the farther shore.

Thus the conscience is enslaved, and then life becomes a scene of continuous sin, binding the chains still tighter around the moral sense till it ceases to remonstrate, and leaves the soul, like the helmless ship, the sport of every wind.

A thrilling instance of the result of such thralldom is thus recorded: "A few years ago, there was living in one of our large cities, a young lady, who was the only child of wealthy and worldly parents. She was fond of the gay pleasures of the city, moved in the highest circles of fashion, and lived as though there was no higher world. While thus living in pleasure, she was asked by a female friend to accompany her to the weekly prayer meeting. There the Spirit of God awakened in her the consciousness of sin, and bowed down her heart in anguish at the thought of her guilt. Her heaviness of spirit was soon discovered at home, and her parents were in consternation lest their beautiful daughter should leave the circles of pleasure for the service of God. They besought her and commanded her to return to the gay world. But a power above theirs was at work, and she was sore stricken in heart. At last, those parents actually bribed her to attend a party of pleasure, by the gift of the richest dress that could be bought in the city of New York. She reluctantly consented, went to the festival, and returned without one trace of her religious emotions. But the joy of her parents was short. In another week their daughter was at the point of death, and the skillful physicians whom they summoned could only tell them that there was no hope. When this opinion was made known to the dying girl, she lay for a few moments in perfect silence, as if surveying the past and looking into the future. Then, rousing herself, she ordered a servant to bring that dress, and hang it upon the post of the bed. She next sent for her parents. In a few minutes they stood weeping at her side. She looked upon each of them for a time, and then, lifting up her hand, and pointing to the dress, said to each of them distinctly, with the terrible calmness of despair, 'Father, mother, there is the price of my soul!'"

Blind to consequences, they were willing to throw the reins upon the neck of vanity, all reckless of the destination whither it would hurry her, and solicitous only that their lovely daughter should ride in splendor on the way. If her prancing steed could have leaped the grave and plunged beyond the hereafter, it might all have been well. But if the terminus of life's road be at the portals of the tomb, rest assured that we shall need an unfettered conscience to pilot us through its gloomy labyrinths. But O, to go there with broken vows staining every remembrance of the past, with fixed habits of sinful indulgence, with a confirmed love of the world, and with an enslaved conscience pressing with fearful weight upon the present—to go there thus burdened and thus haunted! May God save us from the fearful doom.

Again, this habit prevents spiritual progress.

Said an aged minister to his daughter, as she was leaving him just after her marriage, "My child, I want you to remember this one thing, *all you can get out of life is usefulness.*" Noble thought, worthy of a minister of Christ. "*All we can get out of life is usefulness.*" Then the more useful we are, the better do we fulfill our destiny. A useless life in a world where all the tremendous activities of Heaven and Hell are struggling for the mastery, is the greatest inconsistency this side of perdition. A useful life, when every one of its sanctified energies lifts some immortal aspiration into the pure light of Heaven's hope, is the most godlike work this side of heaven.

A listless inactivity, when every influence flows into the balance which poises between two worlds, is disgraceful in the extreme, dishonoring to God, and debasing to humanity. A useful life, in the highest sense, is synonymous with a holy life. And every thing that would prevent spiritual usefulness without, will obstruct the progress of holiness within.

The outer world answers to the inner. A reciprocity of influence pervades both. Repression practiced upon one is destruction to the other. Prevent the streams from flowing out and the fountain will sink within.

If the "mufflers, the bonnets, the mantles, and the wimples, and the crisping pins" help our associates to heaven, then do they also assist our own spiritual advancement. But if good old Bunyan's dream be correct, then is our proposition to the contrary established. "Then I saw in my dream, that when they were gone out of the wilderness, they presently saw a town before them, and the name of that town is Vanity; and at the town there is a fair kept, called Vanity Fair. It is kept all the year long. It beareth the name of Vanity Fair, because the town where it is kept is lighter than vanity, (Ps. lxii: 9,) and also because all that is there sold, that cometh thither, is vanity; as is the saying of the wise 'All that cometh is vanity.' (Eccl. xi: 8, see also i: 2-14; ii: 11-17; Isa. xl: 17.) This fair is no new erected business, but a thing of ancient standing. I will show you the original of it. Almost five thousand years ago there were pilgrims walking to the celestial city, as these too honest persons are; and Beelzebub, Apollyon, and Legion, with their companions, perceiving by the path that the pilgrims made, that their way to the city lay through this town of Vanity, they contrived here to set up a fair; a fair wherein should be sold all sorts of vanity, and that it should last all the year long." "Now, as I said, the way to the Celestial City lies just through this town where this lusty fair is kept; and he that would go to the city, and yet not go through this town, 'must needs go out of the world.' (1 Cor. v : 10.) The Prince of princes himself, when here, went through this town to his own country, and that upon a fair-day too; yea, and, as I think, it was Beelzebub, the chief lord of this fair, that invited him to buy of his vanities, yea, would have made him lord of the fair, would he but have done him reverence as he went through the town. Yea, because he was such a person of honor, Beelzebub had him from street to street and showed him all the kingdoms of the world in a little time, that he might if possible, allure that Blessed One to cheapen and buy some of his vanities; but he had no mind to the merchandise, and, therefore, left the town without laying out so much as one farthing upon these vanities. (Matt. iv: 1-8; Luke iv: 5-8.) This fair, therefore, is an ancient thing, of long standing, and a very great fair. Now these pilgrims, as I said, must needs go through this fair. Well, so they did; but, behold, even as they entered into the fair, all the people in the fair were moved, and the town itself as it were in a hubbub about them, and that for several reasons: For,

"First, The pilgrims were clothed with such kind of raiment as was diverse from the raiment of any that traded in that fair. The people, therefore, of the fair, made a great gazing upon them; some said they were fools; some, they were bedlams; and some, they were outlandish men. (Job. xii: 4; 1 Cor. iv: 9.)

"Secondly, and as they wondered at their apparel, so they did likewise at their speech; for few could understand what they said. They naturally spoke the language of Canaan; but they that kept the fair were the men of this world; so that from one end of the fair to the other, they seemed barbarians each to the other. (1 Cor. ii: 7, 8.)

"Thirdly, but that which did not a little amuse the merchandisers was, that these pilgrims set very light by all their wares. They cared not so much as to look upon them; and if they called upon them to buy, they would put their fingers in their ears, and cry, 'Turn away mine eyes from beholding vanity,' (Ps. cxix: 37,) and look upward, signifying that their trade and traffic was in heaven. (Phil. iii: 20, 21.)

"One chanced, mockingly, beholding the carriage of the men, to say unto them, 'What will ye buy?' But they, looking gravely upon him, said, 'We buy the truth.' (Prov. xxiii: 23.) At that, there was an occasion taken to despise the men the more; some mocking, some taunting, some speaking reproachfully, and some calling upon others to smite them. At last things came to a hubbub, and great stir in the fair, insomuch that all order was confounded. Now was word brought presently to the great one of the fair, who quickly came down, and deputed some of his most trusty friends to take those men into examination about whom the fair was almost overturned. So the men were brought to examination; and they that sat upon them asked whence they came, whither they went, and what they did there in such an unusual garb. The men told them they were pilgrims and strangers in the world, and that they were going to their own country, which was the heavenly Jerusalem,' (Heb., xi: 13–16,) and that they had given no occasion to the men of the town, nor yet to the merchandisers, thus to abuse them, and to let them in their journey, except it was for that, when one asked them what they would buy, they said they would buy the truth. But they that were appointed to examine them did not believe them to be any other than bedlams and mad, or else such as came to put all things into a confusion in the fair. Therefore they took them and beat them, and besmeared them with dirt, and then put them into the cage, that they might be made a spectacle to all the men of the fair. There, therefore, they lay for some time, and were made the objects of any man's sport, or malice, or revenge; the great one of the fair laughing still at all that befell them. But the men being patient, and 'not rendering railing for railing, but contrariwise blessing,' and giving good words for bad, and kindness for injuries done, some men in the fair that were more observing and less prejudiced than the rest, began to check and blame the baser sort for their continual abuses done by them to the men. They, therefore, in angry manner, let fly at them again, counting them as bad as the men in the cage, and telling them that they seemed confederates, and should be made partakers of their misfortunes. The others replied, that, for aught they could see, the men were quiet and sober, and intended nobody any harm; and that there were many that traded in their fair that were more worthy to be put into the cage, yea, and pillory too, than were the men that they had abused. Thus, after divers words had passed on both sides (the men behaving themselves all the while very wisely and soberly before them), they fell to some blows among themselves, and did harm one to another. Then were these two poor men brought before their examiners again, and there charged as being guilty of the late hubbub that had been in the fair. So they beat them pitifully, and hanged irons upon them, and led them in chains up and down the fair, for an example and terror to others, lest any should speak in their behalf, or join themselves unto them. But Christian and Faithful behaved themselves yet more wisely, and received the ignominy and shame that was cast upon them with so much meekness and patience, that it won to their side (though but few in comparison of the rest), several of the men in the fair. This put the other party yet into a greater rage, insomuch that they concluded the death of these two men. Wherefore they threatened, that neither cage nor irons should serve their turn, but that they should die for the abuse they had done, and for deluding the men of the fair. Then were they remanded to the cage again, until further order should be taken with them. So they put them in, and made them fast in the stocks."

Here we have the conduct of the true christian depicted. Reverse the scene and you need no painting to exhibit it. Its original may be found almost anywhere, and mostly because of sinful adornments.

Lastly. The habit of adornment subjects the individual practicing it to the ruinous reaction of personal influence from family companions and from the church.

Take the fashion-loving mother as the first example. Yet how strangely grating sounds that hallowed name in such connection.—Mother!

"The mother in her office holds the key
Of the soul; and she it is who stamps the coin
Of character, and makes the being who would be a savage,
But for her gentle cares, a christian man."

Yet even the mother may so far forget her responsibilities as to throw her molding influence into the scale of worldly pleasure and passing vanity. But, alas! how often does the evil return upon her own head.

A young lady, who had been educated by her mother in the path of folly, was laid upon the bed of death. The past rushed before her with its accumulated load of guilt, and the fearful retributions of the future gathered around her in all the horrors of her wretched state. Her mother strove to comfort her, and spoke of God and mercy. But the daughter interrupted her with the awful exclamation, "It is too late to speak of God to me. You have undone me, and now I am going to hell, and you will come after me." O, what words to be treasured as the dying accents of a child!

How striking the contrast presented by the filial affection of one who had enjoyed a true mother's care, and had felt her holy influence.

"A mother, good and gently kind,
Was there to guide my infant will;
She led my thought, and filled my mind
With memories that linger still.
Many a prayer to Christ her Lord,
She said for me with streaming eyes;
Many a good and holy word,
She bade me learn and ever prize.

"I followed sadly to the tomb
The blessed one that loved me so;
Into the dark and dreadful gloom
To better lands I saw her go.
And with her went the best of joy,
The best of earth, the best of love;
Behind remained the sad alloy
Of colder hearts for me to prove."*

It is related of the ancient Carthaginians, that they had an idol to which they offered their infant children in sacrifice, and which was so constructed that when a child was placed in its arms it would be dropped into a gulf of fire. It was esteemed of much conse-

* From Eaglestone's Poems.

quence that the infant should be presented smiling, and hence the mothers would use every artifice to excite their pleasure, and then with their own hands would place them upon the idol's arms.

We shudder at the fearful recital, and wonder how such unnatural mothers could ever be found.

But they were impelled by religious faith and superstitious fears. The mother who, in a christian land, presents her child a living sacrifice upon the altar of fashion, does so in opposition to all the precepts of her religion, and with none of the constraining influences of devout superstition. But God does not suffer such violations of the holiest relations with impunity. He records his reprobation of them in the avenging strokes of his providence, when some loved but lost child of promise exclaims, "Mother, you have ruined me!" O, fond mother, how could *thy* daughter die?

When the various consequences of the habit of adornment that have been specified in the foregoing pages, are seen in the experience of the members of a family, then follow, as a further result, peevishness, discontent, passionate longings for something still beyond the reach, a fretfulness and fault-finding *snappishness*, all of which change the quiet home into a scene of contention, where the most unlovely traits of character are exhibited. Nor does the evil stop here. Like some demon whom she has called from his repose, but has no power to "lay" again, it follows the victim even to her most retired retreat, and murmurs and dissatisfaction are the aliment upon which she subsists. Again we quote "Nothing to Wear," as exhibiting this result in terms of merited rebuke.

"Oh, ladies, dear ladies, the next sunny day,
Please trundle your hoops just out of Broadway,
From its whirl and its bustle, its fashion and pride,
And the temples of Trade which tower on each side,
To the alleys and lanes where misfortune and guilt
Their children have gathered, their city have built;
Where Hunger and Vice, like twin beasts of prey,
Have hunted their victims to gloom and despair;
Raise the rich dainty dress and the fine broidered skirt;
Pick your delicate way through the dampness and dirt;
Grope through the dark dens, climb the rickety stair
To the garret, where wretches, the young and the old,
Half starved and half naked, lie crouched from the cold;
See those skeleton limbs, those frost-bitten feet,
All bleeding and bruised by the stones of the street:
Hear the sharp cry of childhood, the deep groans that swell

From the poor dying creature who writhes on the floor,
Hear the curses that sound like the echoes of Hell,
As you sicken and shudder, and fly from the door;
Then home to your wardrobes, and say, if you dare—
Spoiled children of Fashion, you've nothing to wear!"

"And oh, if perchance there should be a sphere,
Where all is made right which so puzzles us here,
Where the glare, and the glitter, and tinsel of Time
Fade and die in the light of that region sublime;
Where the soul, disenchanted of flesh and of sense,
Unscreened by its trappings, and shows, and pretense,
Must be clothed for the life and the service above,
With purity, truth, faith, meekness, and love;
Oh, daughters of Earth! foolish virgins, beware!
Lest in that upper realm you have nothing to wear!"

As she is in the family, so is she also in the church. So far as her influence extends, she draws around herself associations of a kindred spirit, and thus transforms the pure and sanctifying atmosphere of the Church of God into stimulus for her own habits of life, at the same time that she repels the more heavenly spirit of the earnest believer.

Thus influence reacts upon its source, perpetuating its streams, and rendering them more copious and murky by every day's experience.

Such are some of the results of the habit

of adornment upon the individual. Of course, we can not expect to see them all exhibited in the experience of every one who is guilty of the practice, for such are the differences of temperament, of circumstances, and of temptations, that they will be varied from the slightest to the deepest shade. But the grand tendency is the same, and the person who dares to brave that tendency is entering the outermost circles of the fearful maelstrom whose revolving tides draw nearer and nearer to their ingulfing center. Happy the one who is aroused ere his giddy brain and accelerated motion preclude the possibility of escape.

Here let me entreat the reader to pause and review the ground. Remember that the consequences to which we have referred do not exist as mere rhetorical points from which to make a case by a process of special pleading. On the contrary, they grow out of the unchanging laws of mind and spirit. As well may any one hope to reverse the most inexorable law of matter, as to enter upon a course of adornment and escape the inevitable entailment which the violated laws of mind impose. Remember, too, that before the God who is the guardian of those laws, the assertion "I do n't believe it," will be no excuse. Disprove it if you can. Reverse the laws of God and change the nature of mind. Enfranchise yourself from the dominion of responsibility. Then, and not till then, can the habit be justified.

CHAPTER III.

ANS. II.—The effect of this habit upon the Church.

It curtails her material resources. Being a voluntary association, her resources are only such as the piety of her membership may place at her disposal. Whatever then militates against the piety of her individual adherents, restricts, to just that extent, the amount of her avails. And if the deteriorating influence be of such a character as not only to depress piety, but also to absorb the means which piety would command, it is all the more powerful for evil.

After all that has been said, the evil influence of adornment upon personal religion can not be deemed equivocal. And its effect upon the material resources of the church is not less clear. It is a fact, which the arithmetic of a child may demonstrate, that if a person has an income of one thousand dollars, and can live on eight hundred, he has two hundred for benevolence and the savings bank. But if his expenses run up to nine hundred and ninety-nine dollars, while his income remains as before, both the savings bank and benevolence will be cheated of their dues. This must be the case even where there is a disposition to give, but when the love of display has eradicated that desire, the cause of Christ must suffer not only present destitution, but prospective embarrassment and want.

Small as the individual deficiencies may be, they swell when taken together, to an aggregate of alarming magnitude. One dollar spent by each member of the christian church for needless ornaments, or for more costly clothing than is actually required, would, if consecrated to the cause of God, pour ten millions a year into his treasury, and send the missionary of the cross to every tribe of man.

"A wise man scorneth nothing, be it never so small or
homely,
For he knoweth not the secret laws that may bind it to
great effects."

These squanderers of the Lord's property fondly imagine that, somehow, the deficiencies of the church must be accounted for by herself, in her collective capacity. They are strangely forgetful that the all-seeing eye distributes to each his personal share in the dereliction, and holds him responsible for it.

It is mournful to think how much remains undone which might be accomplished by the church for the cause of God and the good of man, were all expenditures for unnecessary adornment devoted to his service. There is *surplus* wealth enough connected with the church to-day to endow every institution of learning in the world; to pay the indebtedness of every church; to sustain a missionary in every tribe; to give the Bible to every family who would receive it; in short, to meet all the material necessities of the cause of Christ. This may seem an exaggerated statement, but look at a single fact. The simple *interest* on the possessions of those connected with the churches of our nation alone is about $380,000,000 per year. Add to this the interest on all the rest of the possessions of evangelical christendom, and it will be seen that if our statement is at variance with the truth at all, it falls far short of it.

Why is not this wealth rightly devoted? One main reason is, because Pride and Fashion have forestalled religion, and while they take the munificence, she must rest content with the mere dribblets. Thus God is wronged in the permitted ruin of those who might be saved. And though the laws of man recognize man's right to give or withhold as he pleases, the laws of heaven require that we shall do good as we have opportunity, not merely as we may feel disposed. And this command is just as binding as is the corresponding prohibition of evil. "If thou forbear to deliver *them that are* drawn unto death, and *those that are* ready to be slain; if thou sayest, Behold, we knew it not; doth not he that pondereth the heart consider *it?* and he that keepeth thy soul, doth he not know *it?* and shall *not* he render to *every* man according to his works?"

Again, this habit renders the church exclusive in her privileges.

When the habit of adornment proceeds to its legitimate end, it spreads the tinsel of its trappirgs over every thing, and how shall the proud millionaire, or splendid Miss McFlimsey worship beside the sweat-stained son of toil, or the pale-faced, and finger-worn seamstress? No, no. Brethren and sisters they may be, if they ever reach heaven, but *here* it would be too degrading to have it so. So the pure, free, glorious gospel must be boxed within pews cushioned and carved, must be proclaimed from marble pulpits, (not God's own granite on the hillside,) beneath a frescoed dome, and between painted walls. Its gorgeousness must come, not from the splendid glories of its heavenly surroundings in the rapt visions of a second apostle to the Gentiles, but from the rounded periods and beauteous bouquets of the finished rhetorician. Ye poor, 'twere sacrilege for you to venture there! Dare not the rash attempt. Go, hear the gospel where you may, or where you *can*, but go not there!

"I trod the hallowed ground that bore
 A christian temple tall and proud,
When at each wide and lofty door
 Went streaming in a gorgeous crowd:

A welcome day bade all rejoice—
  A fair and ancient festival,
And the glad organ's mighty voice
  Shook the strong roof and Gothic wall.

"Full many a token marked the fold
  Where rich and high believers meet,
The sacred volume clasped in gold,
  The costly robe and drowsy seat:
Priest, people, altar, chancel, choir,
  Arch, column, window, porch, and gate—
That ample fane, from vault to spire,
  Looked solemn all and calmly great.

"But mark! An old and weary man,
  A stranger clad in raiment vile,
With failing steps and features wan,
  Went tottering up the fair broad aisle:
They cast him out—O, faithless race!
  On some rude bench, unseen, remote—
Convicted in *that* hour and place,
  Of a lean purse and threadbare coat!

"Yes! and if He, who saved the lost,
  Stood fainting on that haughty floor,
Arrayed in weeds of little cost,
  Meek as he sought our world before;
In spite of words which none might blame,
  And works of goodness freely done,
That sordid post of grief and shame
  Would greet Jehovah's only Son.

"Oh, for a prophet's tongue or pen,
To warn the great in wealth and birth,
Who build their God a house, and then
Plant there the meanest pomps of earth—
To brand that church which spurns the poor
From every vain and venal pew,
Where, 'clothed in purple,' herd secure,
To kneel or sleep, the lordly few!

"Give me the shed, low, bare, and plain,
Where love and humble truth abide,
Rather than earth's most noble fane,
Defiled by selfish pomp and pride;
Give me the damp and desert sod,
Walled in by dark old forest trees,
Roofed over by the skies of God;
But perish temples such as these!"

Thus is it that the place which above all others should recognize most constantly the great christian truth that all are brethren, thus it is that the church itself, consecrated to the worship of Almighty God, spurns from her bosom the very classes of society which the Son of God honored with his associations while on earth. True, it may not be an open, verbal rejection, yet it is none the less sure and quite as destructive to her true interests in the world. Exclusiveness in her privileges is too much at war with the essential freedom of salvation, to escape the reprehension of the good, or the cavils of the evil.

"My brethren have not the faith of our Lord Jesus Christ, *the Lord* of glory, with respect of persons. For if there come into your assembly a man with a gold ring, in goodly apparel, and there came in also a poor man, in vile raiment, and ye have respect to him that weareth the gay clothing, and say unto him, Sit thou here in a good place; and say to the poor, Stand thou there, or sit here under my footstool: are ye not then partial in yourselves, and are become judges of evil thoughts?" (James, ii: 1–4.)

Again, this habit destroys her claim to the distinctive character of being separate from the world.

Upon the consistency of this claim rests all her hope of influencing the world to paths of piety. The world is too proud to yield to the demands of christianity, unless there is exhibited incontestibly in her deportment, principles so opposed to every thing selfish, grovelling, and impure, as to demonstrate their heavenly origin. "Come out from among them and be ye separate, and touch not the unclean *thing*," is not merely a command of

God, based upon his authority to institute his own laws, but it is the announcement of a philosophical necessity as deep as the wants of man's nature, and extensive as the relations of the created to the Creator. Whatever then tends to destroy the distinctive marks belonging to the Church of Christ, not only arrays itself against the ordinances of heaven, but stands opposed to the *felt* wants of the human heart.

The church is designed as an aggressive agency, and any alliance with her enemies, or even any suspension of hostilities, is the precursor of defeats. Only in steady, persevering, and unsparing onward movements lies her safety.

It is said that the standard bearer of a Scottish regiment, who was killed at the battle of Waterloo, clasped the colors so fast in death, that a sergeant, after trying to no purpose to rescue them, on the near approach of the enemy made a violent effort, and throwing the dead body, colors and all, over his shoulder, carried them off together. To that brave soldier the loss of his standard was equivalent to defeat. So the church should always look upon any surrender of her outward badges as *disgrace*. Her past history is filled with mournful examples of the truth, that only when "separate from the world," can she successfully prosecute the great work committed to her hands. When the external appearance of the church indicates worldly conformity, she is not far removed from worldly principles. It is an admitted law of nature, that the surroundings of mind shape its development, and often fix its destiny. By the same power of association, the worldly influence that will always gather about the church whose laxity invites their encroachments, will sooner or later cause her to imbibe their spirit, and then her powerlessness and dead formality will be a painted sepulcher that holds but "dead men's bones." Now, behold the progress of the evil. Having curtailed her material resources, and destroyed her chief defenses, it proceeds, with consummate skill, to mine her citadel.

This habit causes her to falsify her professions. Those who compose the church profess that they are "not of the world;" that they are "pilgrims and strangers;" that they seek "a city which hath foundations;" that they are crucified to the world and the world unto them; that they are "dead indeed unto sin, but alive unto God;" that they are laying up "treasures in heaven;" that they are "separate;" that they have "no fellowship with the unfruitful works of darkness;" that they are not "conformed to this world; but transformed by the renewing of" their mind; that they have left all and followed Christ; that they are striving together with him for an incorruptible crown. These are high-sounding professions, but no higher than the genius of christianity authorizes. The world concedes the right of christians to make them, as believers in the gospel, but demands their consistent exemplification. If the life and the profession of christians do not harmonize, the world's confidence is abused, and the injury returns in bitter scorn upon its perpetrators. How often is the reproving exclamation made, "Why such a person is not a christian, she thinks as much of the world as any one." And often not only is the confidence in profession blasted, but belief of religion itself is sapped at its foundations.

A lady, who had been remarkable for thoughtlessness, called for a professor of religion to go with her to visit another professor.

The day passed, and no allusion was made to religion. After taking leave, the gay person said to her companion, "Nothing would have induced me to leave home to-day but the expectation of hearing something about religion, but I have come to the conclusion that there is nothing in religion, or else that my neighbors do not possess it, for if they did, they would speak to me about my soul." In consequence of their deference to the supposed antipathy of their worldly associate, they had not merely lost her respect for them as professors of religion, but had driven away her serious impressions. For she then concluded that if religion was not worth talking about, it was not worth thinking of.

Such is the consequence of worldly conformity in falsifying the professions of the church. Well would it be to heed the warnings of the Savior, "Ye are the salt of the earth: but if the salt have lost its savor, wherewith shall it be salted? It is thenceforth good for nothing, but to be cast out, and to be trodden under foot of men. Ye are the light of the world. A city that is set on a hill can not be hid. Neither do men light a candle, and put it under a bushel, but on a candlestick; and it giveth light to all that are in the house. Let your light so shine before men, that they may see your good works, and glorify your Father which is in heaven." (Matt., v: 13–16.)

As a consequence of the foregoing effect, this habit dishonors the church among those who are without. This is not meant to refer to that contumely and reproach which the malicious love to heap upon everything religious, and which is met by the precept of the apostle, "Having your conversation honest among the Gentiles: that, whereas they speak against you as evil doers, they may by *your* good works, which they shall behold, glorify God in the day of visitation," (Peter, ii: 12,) but to the dignified scorn that men must feel, when they see energies which are professedly consecrated to the service of heaven, prostituted by christians to the debasing work of courting the favor of that world which they theoretically hold at so low an estimate, while they practically elevate it by worldly compliances to the chief place in their affections.

A striking illustration of the effect of such a position was furnished by the conduct of a chief of a native tribe on the Island of Cuba.

The Spaniards had conquered the island and endeavored to force the natives to embrace their religion. This chief was brought to the stake, and *then* exhorted to embrace christianity, that he might be admitted to heaven "Are there any Spaniards in heaven?" asked the indignant chief. "Yes, but they are all good ones." "Then let me die. I can not go to a place where I shall meet even one."

It is true, this is an extreme case, and one resulting from the adoption of extreme measures, but it is the exhibition of *principles common to the human mind*, and which produce results equally decisive and fatal in multitudes of instances. The common sentiment of man is, "We want nothing to do with a religion that will make us no better than we are." Give them a religion whose externals shall shine with the beauty of holiness, and whose manifold character shall challenge the admiration of the world, and they will not be long in rendering the homage of the heart.

Not less does this habit dishonor the character of the church with many of her own members. "There are always some who are liable to be hindered, or turned aside, by such examples. They are conscious that they can not indulge in such things themselves, yet they see almost the whole example of the church against them; and they soon conclude that it is over-righteousness in them to be so scrupulous. They yield; the conscience is enthralled, and they suffer loss, or perhaps go back to the world. Others, seeing such inconsistency, can not admit that the true christian would be guilty of it; and hence denounce all such, as self-deceived, or willful hypocrites; and thus their charity is blasted, and Satan gains a fearful advantage over them. Would it not be well to ask, *not* whether we can practice such things with no injury to ourselves; but "can we do it with no injury to others?" Paul declares such injury to another to be "*sin against the brother, and sin against Christ!*"

"'But take heed lest by any means this liberty of yours become a stumblingblock to them that are weak. For if any one see thee, which hast knowledge, sit at meat in the idol's temple, shall not the conscience of him that is weak be emboldened to eat those things which are offered to idols; and through thy knowledge shall the weak brother perish for whom Christ died? But when ye sin so against the brethren, and wound their weak conscience, ye sin against Christ.' (1 Cor., viii: 9–12.) The facts referred to in this language were as follows. Many of those to whom the apostle wrote, were converted Gentiles. While heathen, they had considered meat offered to their idols as sacred; and, after their conversion, they thought that if such meat were eaten, it must be as sacred to the idol still. Others, who felt that 'an idol is nothing in the world,' regarded such meat as common like other meat, and to be eaten with no more scruples. But the apostle prohibits it, lest 'the conscience of him that is weak' (*i. e.*, who regarded it as sacred still,) 'be emboldened,' etc. We have been thus particular on this passage, because it involves a great principle of equal force in all ages, viz., 'That the lawfulness of men's actions depends not solely either upon the lawfulness of the subject matter, nor upon the conscience of the doers of them, considered in itself, but, *as considered with reference to the conscience of others*, to whom, by the law of charity, they *are bound so to behave themselves*, as by *none* of their actions to give them occasion of sin.' (Stackhouse, Body of Divinity.)

"This principle might be abundantly confirmed by an appeal to other scriptures, were it necessary, but let us make the application. Even granting, for the moment, that this practice is right in itself, and meets the approval of your conscience, still *you have no right to do it if it wounds the conscience of a brother;* for, by so doing, *you 'sin against him, and sin against Christ.'*

"It will not do to demur against this; for *God has said it!* and with him be your quarrel; not with me." (Gift of Power.)

Again, this habit cripples her spiritual resources.

Purity is power—power in its essence, and power in its alliances. Purity, as the aggregate of all christian graces, is the energy of each alone, and of all combined.

If love is power because of its union with Deity; if faith is power because of its divine energies; if sympathy is power because of its hold upon the human heart; if meekness is power because of its essential fitness; if patience is power because of its control of self; if zeal is power because of its momentum; if hope is power because of its inspiration; then purity, the transparent ray formed by the commingled colors of all these graces, is power made up of the blended elements of all its component parts. As the white light of noonday is made up of the seven prismatic colors, and as all these must be mingled in certain proportions, to produce white, so it is with purity. It must be a combination of all the graces, and in certain symmetrical proportions. Mingle the colors in any but the specified proportions, or leave out but one, and you have, instead of the pure white light, some murky tinge. So with purity. Not a solitary grace must be excluded, not one must be in undue proportion, else the effect is spoiled and the labor to that extent lost.

An inharmonious character is always weak for the mightiest purposes of the soul, and an unsymmetrical nature can never be trusted with the widest interests.

Just in proportion then as there is want of development, or an inharmonious development of christian character in the church, in the same ratio is her weakness. She is like an embattled host with too much cavalry—unable to stand the shock; or with too much infantry—unable to pursue an advantage. Whatever else the habit of adornment may do, it is certain to develop an unsymmetrical character, and hence a weak one. And were this a weakness which all tends in one direction, it might be measurably concealed. But its rough and angular points jut out on every side, and present to the sight of the beholder, instead of the beautiful temple which the Prince of architects has planned, a confused pile of huge and unhewn jagged rocks, thrown as if by Titans in mad sport, in one gigantic pyramid of disorder. Its very massiveness may excite wonder, but who will be charmed by its beauties?

In so far as the direct *impression* of the church's externals is concerned, worldly conformity utterly ruins it for good. And then, when the church sues for attention, she comes to the world in the forestalled character of hypocrisy, conscious to herself, and believed by the world. And then, when she pleads, she does it with such an averted eye and a tongue so stammering, that it were better not to plead at all. Such a church dare not look a guilty world in the face and urge them to come to the Christ whom they themselves have forsaken.

Thus the habit of adornment cripples the spiritual energies of the church.

But even give her the vantage ground of an *honest character in the eyes of the world*, while yet this habit is practiced by her members, and still the proposition that she is injured by it remains true. For what can the church do without the Holy Spirit? And is that Spirit to stand at the beck of those who care more for the painted outside than for the "hidden man of the heart?" No, Omnipotence moves when the helpless and trusting penitent cries, or when the pure-hearted believer takes hold of the strength of the Almighty; but the selfish and God-dishonoring professor may lisp his heartless prayers till doomsday all in vain. God's blessings can not be *coaxed* down by a few condescending so-called prayers, formed neither in head nor heart, but uttered by lips that frame flattery more than truth, and speak slander more than love. God will not dishonor his grace by giving it through such a channel. *Purity* is power. Display is hollow-hearted, hypocritical pretense.

The whole of religion is comprehended in two great points, *faith* and *practice*. But *purity* is a condition of faith in the church, and *respect* is a condition of effective practice. Adornment destroys both.

"A gentleman once observed an Indian standing at a window, looking into a field where several children were at play. The gentleman asked the interpreter what was the conversation. He answered, 'The Indian was lamenting the sad estate of these orphan children.' The interpreter inquired of him why he thought them orphans. The Indian, with great earnestness replied, 'Is not this the day on which you told me the white people worship the Great Spirit? If so, surely these children, if they had parents, or any person to take care of them, would not be suffered to be out there playing and making such a noise. No, no. They have lost their fathers and mothers, and have no one to take care of them!'"

Such was the reasoning of the honest-hearted, untutored savage. Similar reasoning has made many men infidels.

CHAPTER IV.

Ans. III. The effect of this habit upon the world.

First. It arms the world with the perpetual and fatal argument from inconsistency.

As there is no surer path to usefulness than a consistent piety, so there is no more certain harvest than inconsistency reaps. The world knows how christians ought to live. They have not read their Bible for nought, and knowing the demands and provisions of grace, they are ready to judge by the rule and plummet. Any failure to reach the Bible standard is condemned with unsparing severity, and every habitual shortcoming is turned by them into a weapon of most effective assault.

The very indulgence which we condemn is the "chiefest of the train," and is all the more destructive as it is perceived to be frivolous and worthless. Not all the arguments which tortured science, or distorted history, or one-sided reason, or bewildered philosophy, or malicious criticism has brought to bear upon christianity, have produced one-half the effect that has resulted from the inconsistency of her professors. It was this that pointed the satire of Voltaire; chilled into icy coldness the philosophic reason of Hume; tipped with bitterest gall the polished shafts of Gibbon's pen, and the wit of Bolingbroke; excited the low scurrility and infamous blasphemy of the miserable and besotted Paine; that, in short, has done more than any other cause to array intellect and honesty against religion. A fact illustrating equally well both sides of this subject is related as follows. "In the town of M——, in New York, there lived an infidel who owned a sawmill, situated by the side of the highway over which a large portion of a christian congregation passed every sabbath, in going to and returning from their place of worship. This infidel was accustomed to manage his mill himself, and having no regard for the sabbath, he was as busy and his mill as noisy on that holy morning as any other. It was soon observed, however, that at a certain time before service, this mill would stop and remain silent, and appear to be destitute of the presence of any human being for a few minutes, then pass on with its noise and clatter till about the close of service, when it again ceased for a little time. It was soon noticed that Deacon B—— passed the mill toward the place of worship, during the silent interval. It appeared that the deacon being (as all other *good* deacons are) regular in his time, the infidel knew just when to stop his mill, so that it should be silent while Deacon B—— was passing, although he paid no regard to the passing of others. On being inquired of, why he paid this marked respect to Deacon B——, the infidel replied, 'The deacon professes just what the rest of you do, but he *lives* also such a life, that it makes me feel bad here,' (putting his hand upon his heart,) 'to run my mill while he is passing.'"

Could the church now have all her membership like this good deacon, how many mills, and tongues too, would cease their clatter, while their possessors, instead of being arrayed under the banners of a jeering infidelity, would be numbered with God's militant host.

Again, this habit excites the suspicion of the world.

Even where the inconsistency, though perceived, does not produce its fruit as detailed in the foregoing remarks, it always excites a suspicion which is ruinous to the influence of the guilty party, and often to the future hopes of the observer. Were human nature pure, it would be prepared to weigh things in the scale of real worth, and hence would not allow a true estimate of one thing to cause an erroneous judgment of another, but as things are, it seems to be a principle of human nature to be suspicious of the *principles* of a theory, when its professed adherents are false to its pretensions. And when once suspicion is aroused, it is easy for it to pass on to other and worse results. "The traveler in Switzerland is shown the thatched roof of a cottage which divides the waters that flow into the Danube and into the Rhine. The little rain that falls on the one side or the other of this roof finds its way either down that dark river which pours its turbid torrent through lands accursed with the yoke of oppression, into the Black Sea, or it swells the tide of that sparkling river that flows on to mingle its waters with the foam-crested waves of the free Atlantic, bearing on its bosom the commerce of free States." So is it in human life.

The narrow line between our consistency and inconsistency, often makes all the difference in the life-journey of those who look to us for examples, between the dark and turbid streams of guilty worldliness and perhaps infidelity, and the bright and joyous one of faith in Christ.

Again, by this habit the world is disgusted, and the authority of the Bible over it is lowered.

"Bad as the world is, it still admires religious principle, and makes the inconsistent professor of it smart beneath the scourge of its ridicule. When we were of the world, we regarded such practices as unbecoming the christian; and, rest assured, the world is no more lenient or erring in its judgment now, than then. The unconverted and the ill-disposed love to make such fashionable professors the scapegoats for their iniquity, and they always intrench themselves behind their defects, for safety from the shafts of conviction or remorse. The church feels this in all her borders, and hence arises the despondent cry, 'We can never prosper with such professors in our midst.' A monstrous wrong is here, and *common honesty* ought to lead such professors to forsake their evil practices or leave the church, that she may no longer be stigmatized by their example." (Gift of Power.) "Lord Rochester told Bishop Burnet that there was nothing that gave him and many others a more secret encouragement in their ill ways, than that those who pretended to believe, *lived* so that they could not be thought to be in earnest." And Frederick the Great, who sneered at all religion, after having promised to promote a certain sergeant when he was pleased with his faithfulness to "his fanaticism," refused to do so when the man had abandoned his religious duties.

Such is the frequent result upon the world of evil-doing in the church. And there is no vice more certain to produce this effect than the habit of adornment, because, while marked with an inconsistency the most glaring, it passes unrebuked, nay, even courted and flattered, by those of whom better things are rightfully expected.

Again, this habit lulls the world to sleep and renders it reckless.

When the power of religion is discarded by its friends, the natural result is that it will be undervalued by the world. Their ears will be calmed by the ever-present opiate of a careless example, while the wild elements of their nature will claim, from the same example, at least a tacit approval, and rush into the extremes of recklessness, because relieved from wholesome restraint. Nor does it take the example of a socially criminal membership to do this. Inconsistency will do as well.

"A mote in the gunner's eye is as bad as a spike in the gun.
And the cable of a furlong is lost through an ill-wrought inch.
There is nothing in the earth so small that it may not produce great things.
And no swerving from a right line that may not lead eternally astray."

The first step taken, it needs only the establishment of a habit of unconcern or recklessness, and then no sound but Gabriel's trump shall wake the soul first led astray by the unfaithfulness of the church.

We hesitate not to affirm that the worldliness of the church is one great cause, yea, the *greatest* cause of infidelity, in the world. True christianity, exemplified in the life, is a thing of such power that it carries the conviction and the demonstration of its divine source with it. Few there are with hardihood enough to deny its origin. But christianity hood-winked, palsied, and caricatured, is the sport of the devil and the scorn of men. Away with the spurious concern, and give us a religion whose exterior shall not brand itself with hypocrisy, and whose outside shall not belie its professions. When the most sacred services of religion are rendered ridiculous by those who professedly reverence and enjoy them, what can we expect but disgust and unbelief on the part of the world, proportioned to their opportunities of observation?

It is upon this ground that the children of pious parents are said to be wilder and more ungovernable than others. The assumption is false, so far as it applies to the children of the truly pious. But the revulsion of feeling from the unquestioning faith of childhood, which loves to reverence what seems to be reverenced by parents, to the chilling conviction of the hollowness of the pretense;—that revulsion which comes just at the age when doubt seems bravery and skepticism manhood, is enough to cut the moorings of almost any youth. I wonder more, in view of this, that the skeptical and profligate are so few than that they are so many.

We will not dwell upon the glaring hypocrisy of standing before the font of baptism, bedecked in all the frippery of fashion, and solemnly vowing to "renounce the devil and all his works, the vain pomp and glory of the world, with all covetous desires of the same," nor will we picture the sickening spectacle presented by troops of regimentaled communicants, marching in laced, hooped, and bedizened grandeur through the "long drawn aisles," wheeling with a sailing sweep before the altar, and then *meekly* (?) kneeling to receive the emblems of the broken body and shed blood of our Lord. Terrible, indeed, must be the moral and mental perversion that sees nothing in such scenes but a "decent regard for appearances," and a "proper respect for the world." If it be possible to paint a panorama, which shall, in one sad view, embody the deepest degradation of the church, and the highest triumph of the powers of darkness, you have it in such life-scenes. [Exhibited in our cities nearly every Sabbath. Admission, gratis—if well dressed.]

Lastly. This habit causes an extravagance, tending to pecuniary embarrassment, dishonesty, perversion of the social instinct, youthful dissipation, domestic broils, conjugal infidelity, a tyrannical and licentious moneyed aristocracy, and a corrupt and venal demagogueism.

Without the strongest evidence we should not dare to name such a fearful array of consequences as chargeable upon any vice. But after all that has been deposed concerning this evil, we have no hesitation in thus grouping many of the worst developments of depravity, and hurling the accusation directly in the teeth of the indulgence. To attempt to prove that it produces extravagance would be insulting to the observation of the reader. And that extravagance produces dishonesty is not surprising when we remember the mental and moral deterioration that is taking place within. When the higher principles of our nature are subjected to the lower, when the moral sensibilities are found in servitude to the passions; when the whole law of interinfluence is tending to moral retrogression, intellectual bondage, and imbecility of the conscience, it would be strange indeed if the multiplied temptations, which the artificial wants excited by extravagance present, did not at last secure a compliance.

> This, above all, to thine own self be true,
> And it must follow, as the day to night,
> Thou canst not, then, be false to any man."

The converse is not less true. If we are *false* to self we may be false to *any;* for the falseness is based upon the same principles. This is, in fact, recognized in the selection of laborers, clerks, and salaried officers, to fill the posts of responsibility in the commercial world. Let the fact be once known that a man is living in a style above his means, and the eye of suspicion is instantly fixed upon him. Defalcations, swindles, robberies, and even murders, may be traced directly to this fruitful source of evil. True, it is not the universal result, but it is a general tendency so frequently reaching its fearful consummation in individual experience, that it should awaken the serious apprehension of every person who may be exposed to its influence.

Our mothers, wives, and daughters, develope our household style and create our necessities, if we would have happy homes. If they abuse their position, the result is most deplorable. A constant fretting for some new adornment or article of display will at last affect the mind of the husband, and put his thoughts upon the rack to devise means to procure the coveted indulgence. He passes from thought to plan, from the plan to its difficulties, and from difficulties to compromises, till the overwhelming desire, made stronger by every hour's consideration, blinds judgment and silences conscience; and then follows the deed of infamy.

The same effect is seen in the youth. His affections are interested; but he can neither secure the object of his choice nor sustain the expenses of a household until gold is his. Strive as he may, the question with him is at last narrowed down to this: "I must give up my hope or get gold." If his mental nature is already perverted by the habit of display, he will probably yield to the temptation; and then speculation, gambling, robbery, or forgery, will be the means selected. If on the contrary, he renounces his hope, the social instincts of his being are crushed, but only to rise with greater intensity, and to reap in illicit pleasures and a dissolute life the harvest which has been sown in extravagance. To so great an extent has this evil reached, that in the city of New York, it has engaged the attention of the public and the press. With the diminished number of marriages, there is a corresponding increase of licentiousness, the effects of which will not stop with the present generation. The children born in such a state of society, the puny offspring of diseased manhood or premature age, will bear in their own sickly constitutions the curse which the law of God visits upon the children for the iniquity of the parents.

Domestic broils, together with consequent conjugal infidelity, are scarcely less deplorable effects. The husband, whose earnings can barely meet the family necessities, must be more than flesh and blood to endure calmly the endless teasing of a worldly wife for new furniture, because some Mrs. Brown has it; or a new dress, because the best has been already worn three times to the same place. Hence come bickering, fault-finding, recrimination, and all the evils to a family growing out of a house divided against itself. At last, the gambling hell, the theater, the assignation house, the common brothel, and the practice of fashionable seduction, follow in the train. Let no one look upon this statement as exaggerated, because of the abominations to which it refers. It sets forth a fact, and a common fact—the legitimate result of the practice of adornment as society is now constituted. Were it not for the blush of modesty, we could relate incidents in illustration which would blanch the cheek with horror, and cause the head to hang for the degradation of humanity. When wives and mothers compound their husband's debts (created by their own extravagances) by compromising their honor with the creditors, or when they sell themselves for the adornments which husbands can not or will not furnish, it is time to speak out concerning the cause of the infamy.

The extravagance of our people has no parallel even in the colossal fortress of aristocratic nations. Queen Victoria dresses less expensively than the wives of our merchants, and the most honored nobility of England expend less for dress and adornment than our own fair dames. As an illustration, it is stated that only last year an American spent $200,000 for a single dress and its adornments for his wife in Paris. Her necklace alone cost $20,000; and, as a legitimate consequence, her husband is now a bankrupt.

Ninety-two per cent. of New York merchants fail or die insolvent; and seventy per cent. of them solely by extravagance. In the year 1856, two and a half millions were lost by this vice in the city and county of San Francisco. Such facts abound to an almost inconceivable extent.

But we turn to mark another tendency of this evil habit.

Its influence upon the young in their selection of companions for life is of the worst description. Instead of allowing affection to direct, money is the oracle whose utterances are regarded as the decrees of fate. Again let us quote "Nothing to Wear."

"So we were engaged. Our troth had been plighted,
Not by moonbeam or starbeam, by fountain or grove;
But in a front parlor, most brilliantly lighted,
Beneath the gas-fixtures we whispered our love.
Without any romance, or raptures, or sighs,
Without any tears in Miss Flora's blue eyes,
Or blushes, or transports, or such silly actions,
It was one of the quietest business transactions,
With a very small sprinkling of sentiment, if any,
And a very large diamond imported by Tiffany.
On her virginal lips while I printed a kiss,

She exclaimed as a sort of parenthesis,
And by way of putting me quite at my ease,
'You know, I'm to polka as much as I please,
And flirt when I like—now, stop, do n't you speak—
And you must not come here more than twice in the week,
Or talk to me either at party or ball,
But always be ready to come when I call;
So, do n't prose to me about duty and stuff,
If we do n't break this off, there will be time enough
For that sort of thing; but the bargain must be,
That, as long as I choose, I am perfectly free,
For this is a sort of engagement, you see,
Which is binding on you but not binding on me.'"

The results of such marriages have been sufficiently depicted above.

There is a universal result of the whole thing, which may now conclude our statement of its evil influence upon the world.

It creates a licentious and moneyed aristocracy, and a corrupt and venal demagogueism.

When money is sought with such maddening energy, for the sake of the gratification which it gives, the feverish craving is not confined to any one class, but from the highest down through every rank of society pours the fearful flood, till from center to circumference, society presents one scene of intense and desperate scrambling after gold, amid the pompous pageantry of fashion-decked dupes and satined buffoons. In such circumstances money is power—power in the hands of the heartless few, whose keener arts or bolder strokes have insured success in obtaining it. And as this effect is developed, the answering tendency in the human bosom to cringe and fawn at the feet of opulence, is exhibited with it, till we have all the elements of our proposition complete in the experience of society. Through the influence of this very cause, our worthiest offices are bought and sold as wealthy demagogues and cringing partizans desire. Well would it be for us to stop and ask ourselves whither we are tending.

Extravagance sapped the foundations of every empire of antiquity, and has ruined more than one of modern date. It is fast blighting our freedom by the corrupted morality of society, and gathering about our own future a cloud of deeper gloom than any other. "If the past has lessons of instruction for us, we may find in the close connection of opulence, the love of display and extravagance, with the rapid decline of national character and strength, in Babylon, Tyre, Sparta, Rome, Spain, etc., the beacon which would warn us of the reefs upon which they were wrecked. This single evil is doing more to undermine our institutions, curtail our benevolence, and limit the salvation of the gospel, than all other causes combined." (Gift of Power.)

Surely every person who feels his interests identified with the good of the race, must look upon all such influences not merely with distrust, but with the abhorrence which they deserve. Nor will he permit his mind to be blinded by the thought that things so small and apparently unimportant in themselves, can not be justly charged with the results detailed in the preceding pages. Reject not the conclusions till you have swept away the arguments upon which they are built. And if perchance they should be found valid, they will furnish but another instance in this world of wonders, when insignificant causes have rolled on to the sublimest or most disastrous results.

We entreat you, then, dear reader, to ponder well the foregoing pages, and endeavor not to silence the voice of reason and conscience in a resort to ridicule, as foolish as it is impotent to shield you from the consequences, both here and hereafter, of rejecting truth.

CHAPTER V.

It is with a feeling of sadness that we approach the conclusion of our work,—not that we are apprehensive of any real weakness in the argument; but we are aware of the deceitfulness of the human heart, and not strangers to the exceeding difficulty of banishing an evil which is fortified by the habits of years, and regarded almost as a household god by thousands of its devotees. Well has one said: "We are not now for the first time to learn that this subject is one upon which it is difficult to touch without giving offense; a hopeless one, perhaps, where the incurable frenzy of the multitude renders the reform, even of the few, a desperate enterprise. What can be said of the morality of *this* fantastic ornament, *that* ridiculous deformity, and the *other* hideous appendage, which would have any weight? It is vain to discuss the moral evil in the fatal constraint applied *here*, and the frightful enlargement made *there*, and the disgusting transformation of God's beautiful workmanship which fashion effects *every where*. It is in vain to appeal to the standard which

God, nature, and common sense have approved. Their opinions on the point are all chaff when they conflict with the decrees of those whom fashion dubs with the magnificent and imposing title of the *world*. The reply to all that is urged is the stereotyped one: 'We may as well be out of the world as out of the fashion.' It is in vain to return for answer, and to *prove* that to be *in* fashion is the readiest way to get *out* of the world. Every man's eye gives ocular demonstration of it. Every member of the medical faculty, at home and abroad, would qualify to the fact under oath. Many a dissection has furnished the proof; many a death-bed of the young and lovely has told the mournful tale; many an early grave has uttered its fearful warnings. What is all this but chaff, when opposed to the despotism of fashion?

"If it were an army of barbarians that had invaded our land, and were cutting off in their bloom the thousands whom God intended to be the mothers of the next generation, we would meet them with well-appointed armies, and send them quickly into the pit; if it were the pestilence, we would fast, and pray, and weep; if it were Christianity herself that demanded one-half of such human sacrifices, the alleged authority of Heaven could not support it against the indignation of pitying humanity, and it would perish amid the cry that would echo from the Atlantic to the Pacific. But lo! since the wide-spreading destruction is dealt out by a few hundreds of the silliest people in Paris and London, the besotted worshipers of this 'goddess of semblance and of shade,' we must submit in silence—and our daughters must die! Religion would have some thing to say in the premises, if her voice were worth listening to. Pity and humanity would speak, if they could be heard; but since their influence can not reach the case, it is to be wished that the pride of Christian women might be invoked. *That* may perhaps save them. A *proper* pride might make them wish to appear comely in the eyes of the other sex. Well, then, let them have the good taste to remain as God made them. God does not make women as Isaiah describes them (chapter iii. 16, etc.), nor the deformities into which modern dressmakers torture them. These are the creations of fashion, which brings every thing into vogue by turns, but good sense, decency, and virtue; and pride, if nothing else, one might suppose, would prompt the modest and virtuous to scorn to imitate fashion's votaries, since those votaries scorn *their* imitation.

"The leaders of the *ton* are running as fast as they can to keep out of the way of the 'vulgar,' whom they despise; and the vulgar are running as fast as they can in the career of imitation, to keep up with the leaders who despise them. Thus, month after month, and year after year, is this preposterous chase kept up, at the expense of countless millions, at the sacrifice of moral principle, time, comfort, health, and life, and to the disgrace of the Christian name: and they that run in this race have, when it ends, *to give an account of themselves to God!* To what conclusion, then, does such a view bring us? It is mad to follow fashion: it may be rash to oppose her; but it is neither rash nor mad to despise her. Let her votaries, if they will, pay to her the passive and implicit service which she exacts; but Christian women should scorn to follow their lead, and renouncing this despicable and hurtful vanity, take care to dress, as well as conduct themselves, with the simplicity and gravity which become their purer character and diviner hopes."—(Protestant Churchman.)

Would to God this appeal might prove successful! Surely an evil that paralyzes almost every arm, and palsies the energy of nearly all good influence, and threatens at no distant day to obliterate all the landmarks of vital "Christianity, must be of sufficient magnitude to awaken the earnest solicitude of every true lover of the sacred cause. Were it confined to a small locality, or to a single class, it might be uprooted, or at least curtailed in its progress, and restrained in its influence.

"But pervading, as it does, all places, and commanding the hosts of every rank, it spreads its tides of desolating worldliness wherever the cross casts its shadow, and triumphs *most* within the sacred precincts of God's own sanctuary. Its upas breath is every where instilling its subtile poison into the life-current of the young convert, and transforming his warm, active zeal, and earnest prayers, and burning love, into the cold, apathetic breathings and fitful starts of this charnel dream land of his soul: and it calls the myriads of modern Israel to dance around the Golden Calf of their own making, while their offended God from Sinai beholds their base ingratitude. O! 'when will he arise to shake terribly the earth?'

"But the remedy! Where is that? Chiefly, fellow Christians, *in you!* The Church authorities may, and ought to do some thing *to prevent all such accessions to her membership hereafter;* but they already swarm within her pale. Let your light shine. Be the first to renounce the unhallowed practice, and ere long the sacred leaven will work out through the masses of the Church and purify the whole. Ministers here have a most solemn duty."—(Gift of Power.) Yet who of these ministers has lifted up his voice like a trumpet, and showed Israel their transgressions and the house of Judah their sins?

To you, O man of God, I make my first appeal; and it shall be in the language of Him who sent thee:

"Son of man, I have made thee a watchman unto the house of Israel: therefore hear the word at my mouth, and give them warning from me. When I say unto the wicked, Thou shalt surely die; and thou givest him not warning, nor speakest to warn the wicked from his wicked way, to save his life; the same wicked *man* shall die in his iniquity; but his blood will I require at thine hand. Yet if thou warn the wicked, and he turn not from his wickedness, nor from his wicked way, he shall die in his iniquity; but thou hast delivered thy soul. Again, When a righteous man doth turn from his righteousness, and commit iniquity, and I lay a stumbling block before him, he shall die: because thou hast not given him warning, he shall die in his sin, and his righteousness which he hath done shall not be remembered; but his blood will I require at thine hand. Nevertheless if thou warn the righteous *man*, that the righteous sin not, and he doth not sin, he shall surely live, because he is warned; also thou hast delivered thy soul."—(Ezek. iii: 17-21.)

From the pulpit and the altar I turn to fathers, husbands, brothers, sons. Regard not this thing as unworthy of your attention. There is not a financial project known to man; there never has been an economical plan proposed by statesmen; there can not be found a remedy for a pecuniary evil, whether national, social, or individual, which can compare in importance with a scheme which would remove this deep-rooted, universal curse. I saw a friend driving a span of splendid bays. I asked him what they cost him. "Eighteen thousand dollars." "Why, how is that?" "Well, when I sold my old horses and bought these, my harnesses and carriage did not correspond: bought new. Then my barn was too shabby for such a team: built new. Then my house was too poor beside my barn; so I built a new house. Then the old furniture would not do. So, altogether, my span has cost me eighteen thousand dollars." This only illustrates the general principle which runs through every item of expenditure in social life.

But fathers, husbands, pardon me, for in the moneyed aspects of the case, I have neglected these purer, holier, more tender relations recognized in the very names by which I address you.

O father, those lovely daughters, whose smiles are sunshine to thy burdened spirit, and whose light-hearted gleefulness drives dull care away, those daughters are even now exposed to the fearful evils which have been depicted in the foregoing pages. Whether they realize it or not, they have a right to demand protection from your hands. Yea, their very loveliness does plead for your jealous watchcare, as only the tender endearments of such relations can plead. And you, doting husband, would you save the gentle disposition of your loving wife from being soured and spoiled, then assist her in the battle against this omnipresent evil. For rest assured that she will need your word of approval and encouragement.

To *philanthropists* of every class the subject appeals with an earnestness of utterance intensified by its neglect.

The development of other evils may be more glaring, and hence may attract most of your attention. But this is all the more dangerous, because so secret and unsuspected. Do you believe the conclusions established in this book? Then, in the name of humanity, bestir yourselves. Strike at the root. Sound the tocsin of alarm. Arm an exterminating crusade. Down with the foe of our hearthstones, our hearts, and our souls.

The woman who is not by very nature a philanthropist is an unnatural creation. Here, then, in making our appeal, we expect an audience. O ye who bear the blessed name of mother, listen while we plead. One who responded to that call once knelt with her little boy in prayer. Ere he had seen his eighth summer she died. But in after life her pure spirit watched over him, and at last led him to the cross. He became a minister, and by his labors Claudius Buchanan, one of the apostles of missionary effort in India, and the instrument of awakening *Judson* to the wants of India, was converted. Scott, the commentator, and Wilberforce, the champion of African freedom, and the author of that "Practical View of Christianity," which made Legh Richmond a christian, were both led to Christ by him. That boy was the Rev. John Newton, and that young matron, whose early efforts thus gloriously prospered, was his mother. Mark here the workings of that great law of interinfluence to which we have so often alluded.

In 1798, a vessel bound to sea was detained near the Isle of Wight by a change of wind. The Rev. Mr. Crabb, a Wesleyan chaplain, went on shore, and preached from the text, "Be ye clothed with humility." It was the word of life to Elizabeth Walbridge, the "Dairyman's Daughter." Legh Richmond wrote her memoirs, and they have been instrumental in saving hundreds, beside raising up three entire churches in Armenia. And still the work goes on. O what a result from a mother's prayers!

Mother, behold thy influence, and remember it is equally as potent for evil as for good. The Jewish mothers sacrificed their jewelry for the temple at Jerusalem. Even the heathen women of Ephesus gave their ornaments for a temple to Diana. Shall it be said that you love Christ less? Shall the noble purposes of infinite mercy be defeated for want of woman's sympathy? Shall this habit of adornment, the foundation of all worldly conformity, be suffered to spread itself abroad for want of your efforts?

If these considerations do not move you, at least for the sake of self-preservation, arouse yourselves from this stupor. Can you, dare you, face the responsibilities of life with such a sin eating away your piety, destroying your self-respect, and ruining you for the future? You may say you can not believe so many good christians would indulge in the practice if it is such a sin. But this is begging the question. It is making the single fact of their inconsistency a sufficient rejoinder to all the evidence that has been adduced, as well as overlooking the fact that there have been in darker days rum-drinking christians and patriarchal polygamists. But now the light shineth, and if now you trim to the world you deliberately balance probabilities of eternal ruin, and invoke the doom of those against whom Sodom and the queen of the south shall arise in judgment, for sinning in greater light and against greater grace.

Beside all this, if not convinced now, no power of logic and no array of facts would convince you. Few doctrines of your creed, whatever it be, have ever been presented to your mind with an equal amount of evidence. And the mental injury which must result from a willful blindness to such testimony can scarcely be appreciated.

Surely, the young, the lovely, the sympathizing will not deny their aid. Especially the young christian, in the fervor of first love, will not refuse to sacrifice for Christ.

Now look upon the sin. It squanders the means; misspends the time; perverts the judgment; cultivates selfishness; corrupts the will;

excites the passions; chills the sympathies; hardens the heart; degrades the mind; violates vows; increases love of the world; creates habits of sinful indulgence; enslaves the conscience; prevents spiritual progress; and exposes to the ruinous reaction of its influence.

All this for the individual.

For the church. It curtails her resources; destroys her claims; falsifies her professions; dishonors her character; cripples her energies; and renders her exclusive in her privileges.

As respects the world. It arms it with the fatal argument of inconsistency; excites suspicion; creates disgust; renders reckless; lulls to sleep; and encourages an extravagance which produces pecuniary embarrassment, dishonesty, perversion of the social instincts, youthful dissipation, domestic broils, conjugal infidelity, a tyrannical and licentious moneyed aristocracy, and a corrupt and venal demagogueism.

Have these conclusions been established? If not, which have failed, and where is the weakness? I beseech you act intelligently upon this subject. What more can be needed, —nay, what more could be furnished to show the utter, intrinsic, unchanging hostility of this indulgence to the cause of Christ and humanity?

Inaction is assent to the crime. Compromise is treachery to heaven. Willful rejection of the truth is eternal ruin. What, then, will you do? Whatever you do, remember that tastes are so variable that no standard can be fixed for all except the simple one of *exclusion:* "Whose adorning let it not be," etc.

First of all, divest yourself of the indolatrous appendages. Then, if you wish to exchange them for a treasure in the heavens that failed not, you can do as did a wealthy and refined lady who heard a portion of this essay read in manuscript. She sent for a minister and gave him her ornaments to be sold for the assistance of the poor.

Christ and humanity plead. Reader, what shall be thy response?

www.ingramcontent.com/pod-product-compliance
Lightning Source LLC
LaVergne TN
LVHW011237110826
845150LV00006B/1661

* 9 7 8 1 4 2 5 5 1 3 5 6 6 *